The Single-Again Man

THE SINGLE-AGAIN MAN

by

Jane K. Burgess, Ph.D.

Foreword by John DeFrain, Ph.D.

Lexington Books

D. C. Heath and Company • Lexington, Massachusetts • Toronto

Library of Congress Cataloging-in-Publication Data

Burgess, Jane K.
The single-again man.

Includes index.
1. Single men—United States.   2. Widowers—United
States.   3. Divorced men—United States.   4. Single
fathers—United States.   I. Title.
HQ800.B87   1988   305.3'890652   86-46342
ISBN 0-669-15675-2 (alk. paper)

Published simultaneously in Canada
Printed in the United States of America
International Standard Book Number: 0-669-15675-2
Library of Congress Catalog Card Number: 86-46342

The paper used in this publication meets the minimum requirements of
American National Standard for Information Sciences—Permanence
of Paper for Printed   Library Materials, ANSI Z39.48-1984.

∞™

ISBN 0-669-15675-2

88   89   90   91   92   8   7   6   5   4   3   2

To my son,
DAVID B. BURGESS, M.D.,
*and to all the gentlemen whose contributions
made this book possible.*

Contents

Foreword

John DeFrain

ERE is a wonderful book! A book about the intimate lives, the intimate experiences of men in our society.

If you want to understand a man best, see how he responds in a crisis. And the men who tell their stories in these pages are responding to one of life's greatest traumas—the separation or loss of their wives through death, divorce, or physical or mental breakdown.

Dr. Jane Burgess, the author of this book, has done a masterful job of weaving the men's stories into a very useful book for husbands grieving over the loss of their spouses. Burgess is a seasoned researcher, a sociologist at the University of Wisconsin-Waukesha who has been studying the hard times human beings face for many years.

She has written a moving, perceptive, and positive book on how men cope with being single again. She is an excellent writer. But perhaps Dr. Burgess' greatest gift is that of an interviewer. She sat down with dozens of bereaved men, looked in their eyes, and listened to their hearts. What they told Jane will make you laugh and cry, and amaze you at their strength and sensitivity.

For, in short, men aren't all that bad. We have been told for the past 20 years, and rightly so, that some men are hard-nosed, insensitive, and brutal. Researchers have uncovered the dark side of the American male, the heavily defended ego that stifles natural emotion and hides behind a mask of *machismo*.

Jane has gone deeper, underneath the mask of control. She has gone deep into the heart and soul of these good men in her book, and she introduces us to what is perhaps closer to the truth: that deep down, good men are very much like good women. They are kind, warm, sensitive, caring, and emotional. And they grieve and experience the pain of their spouses' loss in the same way women do—all the way to the marrow.

What are men really like inside? Stripped of all their defenses, we see the *real* man in Jane's book, and he often sounds just like a woman talking. For in fact, men and women are much more alike than different. They are, in essence, all *human*.

This book, then, serves two major purposes: To help the grieving man transcend his grief and learn to live again, and to educate and prod our society into action. In sum, we need to "provide men in our society the same sympathy, empathy, and emotional support offered women when they face a situation too traumatic to be handled alone."

Amen, Jane. Amen.

Acknowledgments

I AM most grateful to the wonderful men who shared the details of their lives as single-again men so as to lighten the pain for others. I have changed names and details to protect their privacy.

It is impossible to name all those who sustained me in my efforts to write this book, but I wish to express my sincere gratitude to those who provided special assistance: Paula Dail, who supplied many contacts for interviews; John DeFrain and Nick Stinnett, who, in addition to their kind support of my efforts, provided me with the first opportunity to present my findings on widowed and divorced men at a University of Nebraska-Lincoln Family Strengths Conference; my editor, Carolyn Kott Washburne, who provided invaluable assistance in editing and putting this manuscript together; and Lynn Paque, for her excellent typing of the manuscript.

And to my mentor, S. Robert Reiber, who inspired me to undertake this book, my deepest gratitude.

Introduction

THE popular misconception about newly single men is that not only do they have a relatively easy time adjusting, but many also enjoy "sportier" lives than when they were married. Unburdened from day-to-day responsibilities for home and family, they have ample opportunities for socializing and sex.

The reality, however, is that many newly single men have difficulty living through the immediate changes in their lives and coping with the enduring effects of their loss. Living in a barren apartment, separated from friends and having limited access to his children, the "typical" newly single man lives a life that is far from glamorous.

Each year in the United States approximately 250,000 men join the ranks of the newly divorced, widowed, or separated. Most of them suffer the same pain and isolation that newly single women do. Yet men have nowhere near the support system available to women to get through problems of widowhood or divorce. Widowed, divorced, and separated men agree, "I am expected to handle my feelings all on my own." Bob, a forty-year-old widower with three young children, says, "When I went back to work, the attitude seemed to be that I had buried my wife last week, and this week I would be out looking for a date. No one would talk with me about my wife's death."

When a marriage ends, for whatever reason, most men go through a painful period, feeling that their whole world has been turned upside down. Yet compared with the many books written to help newly single women to adjust to the changes taking place in their lives, men have been ignored. Among the many questions unanswered are: How does a man react when his wife tells him she no longer wants him, or when his wife dies? Where can he turn for help? If he has custody of children, how will he manage the many situations his wife usually handled? If he does not have custody, how will he remain close to them? What about his social life? His sexual needs? How will he cope with the lasting effects of divorce, separation or death to achieve a sense of wholeness?

To find answers, I asked twenty-five divorced or separated men and twenty-five widowers to talk with me about their feelings and experiences as single-again men. The occupational status of these men varies from professionals to skilled laborers. They vary in age too, the widowers being older, generally, than the divorced and separated men. This book is based primarily on their biographies.

There are major differences in the impact of a loss depending on how it occurs. Men whose wives initiate divorce, for example, have quite different reactions and emotions than men who initiate divorce themselves. Likewise, the reactions to death are different for men whose wives die suddenly or unexpectedly than for men whose wives die after a lingering illness. Men involuntarily separated from their wives by disability are in limbo—they have wives, yet they don't.

Despite their differences, however, newly single men share many of the same problems. More than half the widowers who contributed to this book still have children in their care, and 10 percent of the divorced men have custody of their children. These men are struggling to adjust to life as single parents and at the same time re-establish their own identities as singles.

The stereotype of the dashing single-again man is especially problematic for those who are ready to establish new social relationships. Conflicts about sexuality, how to cope with feelings about sex when beginning to think of dating and what to do about sexual needs are discussed at length.

Finally, professionals and lay people alike have begun to recognize that grief is as much a part of the process of divorce or involuntary separation as it is the process of death. What is not recognized as readily is that most men cannot handle the loss of a spouse, under whatever circumstances, easily or alone.

It is my wish that this book give comfort and hope to widowed, divorced, and separated people, and to those close to them. As I talked with single-again men about their grief and adjustments, I was impressed with their willingness to help others. Knowing these generous men trusted me to report their stories in an honest, forthright manner has been inspirational.

1

Newly Single Men: Their Differences and Similarities

W HAT are the immediate reactions and problems newly single
men experience in adjusting to the loss of a marital relationship? The immediate reactions differ, as do coping skills, and
depend upon many factors, including the quality of the marital
relationship, the availability of professional help, the amount of
support they receive from family and friends, individual personality
traits, the presence or absence of children, and the way in which the
separation from their wives occurs. But whether a man is widowed
or divorced, he feels many of the same emotions of shock, anger,
sadness, panic, and guilt.

Being alone is not a particularly happy state for most newly single
men, and they typically find adjusting to their loneliness very
difficult. The problem is often compounded by several factors: first,
ours is a paired society with no clear-cut traditions or customs about
how to behave toward people who are no longer married. In
addition, there is a widespread myth that men can handle any
personal problems easily and with no help. Finally, an even more
devastating factor is the stereotype that plagues these men—that
they are sporty, half-crazed sex maniacs. In reality, most newly
single men feel as Marty, a thirty-year-old recently divorced man,
describes, "I don't particularly relish 'single life in a double bed'
whether women believe this or not. A man is not always looking for
sex—he sometimes wants a sense of intimacy, friendship, companionship."

Is it more difficult to cope with the death of a wife or the loss of a wife through divorce? The following provides some insights.

The Divorced Man

When we discuss divorced men, we must first ask, "Who initiated the divorce?" It is clear that a man whose wife initiates the divorce has a more difficult time accepting and coping with the aftermath of his divorce than does a man who initiates the divorce himself, or where it is a mutual decision.

The divorce process is different depending on which partner is being divorceed. Typically, a man who wants a divorce feels a strong need to get out of the relationship, although he may still care for his partner. Their sexual relationship has probably waned. He feels troubled about hurting his wife, but knows he needs time and space for himself. He may have undergone therapy, seeking a way to prepare for the change. He decides that remaining together would be destructive to himself and his wife. He ends the relationship by telling her the truth.

After the divorce, he feels a tremendous sense of euphoria and freedom. Later, when he begins to feel disapproval from friends and family for what he has done, he will be uncomfortable with his single-again status. He resents that people consider him the "bad guy," without any understanding of his marriage. He feels lonely. However, he generally overcomes his negative emotions and begins to enjoy his freedom.

The man whose partner initiates the divorce typically argues that he did not know anything was *that* wrong with the marriage—that given a chance, and time, he would change, would make everything okay. He is completely unprepared for a separation and delays working through the divorce process, hoping for a reconciliation. He usually despairs, and may feel devastated. He may be consoled by his family and friends who feel he has been wronged. It is important that such a man go through the grief process to overcome his feelings of rejection. He must find ways to rebuild his shattered self-esteem so that he gains self-confidence and feels free to date—to build a new, happier life.

We will consider first men whose wives initiate divorce, followed by men who initiate divorce. Finally, we will consider men who jointly decide upon a divorce.

Men Who Are Left

Men whose wives initiate divorce suffer extreme emotional pain. They express feelings of rejection, shock, helplessness, disbelief, betrayal, resentment, denial, despair, and loneliness. They are unable to concentrate on anything. They feel out of control and depressed, and they hate to be alone. Their self-esteem drops considerably. Some still love their wives. Most do not want the divorce.

As Miles, a thirty-eight-year-old teacher says, "After nine years of marriage, her suggestion of a divorce was a complete surprise. She never told me what she didn't like about me. I was shocked— speechless. I was still in love with her. I was angry when she just left me and took the kids with her. The loneliness was horrible. I began doing crazy things when my emotions were out of control, like getting drunk and spending the night with a pick-up. My heartache was like a physical thing, like having my insides grabbed and twisted. The pain went right up into my throat and stayed there."

Other men in his situation echo Miles' sentiments. Few believe their marriages are unsalvageable. An exception, however, is Warren, forty-eight, a university professor who speculates that the long-term problems in his marriage began with his having a totally different social background, interests, and education. "It was difficult for her to move into my social and family circle," he says. "But after twenty-one years of marriage, I thought she was managing.

"Our marital relationship was very unsatisfactory to both of us, but because we had children, and I thought they needed me, I would not consider divorce. When she first asked me to leave, it was during the time that I was having an affair, which was probably my subconscious way to get out of this marriage. I didn't have the guts to leave, so I had an affair so that she would kick me out. I was frightened of a divorce.

"When she asked me to get out, I experienced terrible feelings of anger—anger at myself for getting into this mess in the first place. I was very bitter at my lot, but I had always rationalized that she was a good woman and I had to stay because of the children."

George, too, felt his marriage was unsatisfactory. "My wife was never very clear except she couldn't stand being married to me any longer. She never accused me of anything specific. Part of it was that she is very competitive. We are in the same profession, and I am way ahead of her—that bothered her.

"I really thought our marriage was bad in the sense that there was no emotional warmth, little or no sex, and the communication was poor. Surely there should be more to married life than having a wife who spoke to you only as a professional colleague about her work and career. I did not want a divorce, due to my concern for our child and for financial reasons. Living separately, neither of us could continue our style of life. So even though I felt our marriage was rotten from the beginning, I probably would have done nothing to end it. She sued for a divorce, finally."

The majority of men who don't think their marriages are bad enough to divorce or who don't divorce despite a poor relationship do agree their sex lives are poor. Some have wives who are "chasing around" or who have fallen in love with another man. Most are told they are no longer loved.

There are many reasons for wanting to break up a marriage, as Jim found out. Jim is a forty-two-year-old engineer whose wife left him for an unusual reason—she changed her sexual preference. After nine years of marriage, his wife told him she no longer wanted to live with him. "It seemed as though everything was fine one day, and the next day she decided she wanted me out of her life," he says. "I knew we had some minor problems. Our sex life was gone, for she had no interest in it even though I could never get her to talk about her sexual feelings. I was still very much in love with her, and having her leave me for a lesbian lover was too much for me to take.

"It was a total shock. I wondered if it was my fault that she preferred a woman. But there was no way I could change that. I wasn't any good for her because I was a man. It was a real blow to my ego. My emotions were definitely out of control. I didn't have anybody to talk to, and my only real friends were a thousand miles away. I wrote her hundreds of letters after she left, but I never mailed them. I wanted her to be like she was before, which was asking the impossible. She could never be that way again, and I missed the person who wasn't there any more. She hadn't died, she had just changed—turned into a different person. I felt such heartache. I frequently contemplated suicide. My life was shattered. The whole thing was so painful. This pain is just beginning to lessen after six months."

For men whose wives initiate divorce, grief symptoms are very similar to those that widowers endure. They are hurt, afraid, and lonely, wondering, "Why me?" They may suffer loss of appetite, have trouble breathing, and dwell constantly on their loss. These men suffer a terrible sense of rejection. They consider themselves worthless, unloved, and unlovable.

Men Who Initiate Divorce

Men who initiate divorce are not spared negative emotions, although the divorce is not nearly so devastating psychologically. They do not feel rejected or unworthy. They may be angry, but primarily at themselves for delaying divorce so long. Often they feel deep guilt, but also relief, freedom, and escape. While happy to be getting out of a bad marriage, all experience loneliness for a time.

Richard, a professional man at age sixty, says, "I felt a lot of bitterness and repressed anger at our relationship and my wife's behavior. I felt guilty over kicking in the sand castle, for now our house is being sold and the kids will have to live elsewhere. I feel guilty for not dealing more adequately with my marital relationship for I know I was half the problem. I do feel a great sense of relief that I have taken action to get out of the marriage."

Many of these men described their wives as either terribly dependent upon them, to the point that they felt stifled or trapped, or domineering, showing them little respect as a person or as a productive wage-earner. John, a highly successful industrialist who is now divorcing his wife of fifteen years, says, "My wife is an educated woman, very capable in her professional endeavors. Yet with me she played the dependent role to keep me captive. She made no decisions without asking me for assistance, whether it was what dress to wear or which brand of cereal to purchase. She insisted on togetherness to the point of driving me to distraction. If I did make a move without her, she questioned me for hours until she was satisfied that she had learned every possible detail." John knew he should have resisted this dependency years ago and he often thought of a divorce. But it seemed easier to put up with it, and he became a workaholic. He built up a profitable business, which he owns. He and his wife never had children, and they had no sexual relationship for years. To escape boredom, they traveled—he and his wife have traveled around the world twice.

John's situation became further complicated when he met someone he wants very much to be with. "Four years ago I met my one and only true love. She is widowed and loves me as I love her. It's as though the years in between have evaporated, and it is just as it was when we were two youngsters—madly, passionately, ecstatically in love. Finding each other again is like a beautiful miracle to us.

"This woman offers all the love, affection, and sex that I have so sorely missed in my marriage. She is an independent woman, self-assured, highly successful in her profession. She truly believes that love involves freedom to be one's self. She would never be possessed by anyone, nor would she try to possess me as my wife has done.

"For over three years I have suffered feelings of guilt and anger—wanting freedom to marry Jean and yet not wanting to hurt the woman I have been married to for forty-five years. I feared the changes that would take place in my life, the accusations from our friends, the anguish, the pain and bitterness that goes with divorce. Breaking up a marriage is contrary to my religious and moral convictions. I feel anger at the frustrations I have endured and anger at myself for the long delays in taking the initiative to obtain a divorce. Guilt, too, for causing Jean anxiety and despair over my years of vacillations, over my confusion. I needed to realize that living with a woman I did not love was destructive to myself, my wife, and the woman I desire to marry. I found my strength to end my marriage when I learned to love myself sufficiently to feel that I deserved much more out of life than a dull, empty, frustrating marriage."

John is finally in the process of divorce and is in therapy to help give him direction and help him handle his guilt and anger. "I have learned to let my conscience guide me but not control me," he said. "I am not lonely as many divorced men seem to be, for I do have Jean, who is standing by my side, waiting to become legally mine."

Samuel, a fifty-five-year-old physician, was not married to a "clinging vine" as John was. Rather, his wife was a domineering woman who had to have the last word in everything. He begins by saying, "She never respected me either as a person or as a physician. The initiative to leave was mine. Ours was really a dead marriage. Essentially, we were living together as roommates, but nothing more. No sex. No affection. No communication. No kind of interpersonal relationship. I was always being told, 'You don't do it that way,' or 'Do it this way.' She was the expressive one, I was introverted, and a combination of the stress we felt with our marriage and the inability to deal with it precipitated my decision to get out of this unsatisfactory alliance.

"Getting a divorce is a little like an operation. It's lucky you don't know all that is going to transpire when you start out. I don't regret the decision even though it is certainly harder than I anticipated. It's going to take a lot longer to process the divorce, too, than I ever thought possible.

"The struggle with my self-identity is also a problem. I can't think of myself as a 'me.' I continue to ask myself, 'Who am I?' I need to put myself as number one and to develop a sense of self-love. My wife, never giving me respect as a person, contributed to a poor self-image. I must change a few attitudes about myself to begin with, but I find this change a very long time in coming. Every time I do something on my own which I did for twenty-five years as part of a couple, it's a new shock. But at least I now can choose my own movies rather than being dragged out of the house to see what my wife wanted to see. It's a wonderful feeling, being in control of myself."

Roger, a thirty-eight-year-old recently divorced college professor, also initiated his divorce. His wife, similar to Samuel's, was domineering, and he had other reasons for his decision. "My wife was very dogmatic and insisted that things be done her way. She always saw either black or white, and I could see the gray. I had hoped things would change during the course of our marriage, but they didn't. I felt trapped, and eventually I decided I had made plenty of changes her way and she hadn't given in in any way. I just felt things had to change and she wasn't about to change. I felt restrained and dissatisfied with my life."

Sexual problems started early in Roger's marriage. His wife began to gain weight and ended up, at five feet tall, weighing more than two hundred pounds. "Frankly, I did not enjoy going to bed with her, and our sex life was very unsatisfying," he said, "but this was partially my fault. We got married when we were very young, and I was pretty inexperienced and inept, so we didn't get things going right from the beginning. Our biggest problem was her easily aroused temper, and when things went wrong with our sex, instead of being willing to talk things out, she would get mad and make ugly, disparaging remarks about my sexual performance.

"I understand in retrospect that she felt embarrassed about her weight, and the only way she could handle it was to get angry at me. She can be so funny and a little humor could have gone a long way with helping our sex life. She had humor in other things, but hell, she had no humor at all when it came to sex. What I can remember in those circumstances is her shouting from the bedroom that it was time for me to go in there and perform. That was ten years ago. I strongly feel that you cannot order a man to perform. A woman should try to make sex interesting, too, and her actions were entirely the wrong kind of approach. I just avoided having sex with her."

Roger says there is no one telling him he is doing everything wrong all the time. He is proving to himself he can get along. "I feel a hell of a lot better about myself now. This has been a time of great growth and self-improvement for me," he says. "Actually, one should look at divorce as an opportunity to find a whole new world out there. It can be pretty damn nice, but it's up to the person to find it."

"Depression was something I was terrified of, and it never happened to me. There have been times when I felt a little bit low or scared, especially around the time of the divorce trial, which was quite a mess. But I think depression is something you can let yourself fall into, and if you decide you are not going to let it happen, you can avoid it."

He concludes, "I think divorce is, unfortunately, a way of life. I suppose, like marriages, there are good divorces and bad ones. I don't know what you can do to make a divorce good, because by the time a marriage breaks up they are what they are. The partners are either reasonable adults and can do it with a minimum of bitterness, or they are not."

Quite often people develop the attitude toward the man who initiates divorce as cruel, inconsiderate, and heartless, leaving his wife for no legitimate reason or perhaps because he has found himself a young, sensuous sex partner. Many men dread this stereotype. "What will my friends and family think? They will probably all hate me," is a frequent fear.

Men seek divorce for many reasons: a wife's over-dependency or over-dominance; a wife's inability or refusal to compromise; lack of love, affection and sexual satisfaction; a realization that things will never get better; constant bickering and fault-finding; and meeting someone who could fill needs for love and for sex. Some older men leave when their children are grown and no longer need a father's constant attention, while men with younger children also divorce, feeling that divorce is better for their children than living in a hostile, hateful environment.

A Joint Decision To Divorce

A joint decision to divorce by no means precludes psychological pain. Many men who agree with their wives that divorce is necessary speak of feelings of rejection as they realize they are no longer desired as husbands. They feel frustration and anger for not having realized the inevitability of divorce sooner. There is guilt over having subjected their children to the anguish and fear caused by divorce. And there is loneliness for most of them as they are shut out from their homes and families.

Carl, a forty-five-year-old electrician, has been divorced just two days when he talks about the joint decision to end his marriage of twenty years. "We talked it over for a long time, and although I wanted to delay the final separation, we decided we should divorce. We agreed on everything, and the divorce went as smoothly as one can go. The emotional upheaval which I felt throughout the divorce process has not been as great as I expected. I guess, though, I have been mentally divorced from my wife for quite a while because deep in my heart I knew our marriage was over five years ago."

After ten years of marriage, four children and three moves, Carl and his wife had bought a home in the suburbs. Things seemed to be going well. They never fought. Carl now realizes they never communicated much about anything, and it was the breakdown in communication that hurt them. There was no cheating, no back-stabbing—they just grew apart.

"We have seen many unhappy people staying together for the sake of the kids, but it just doesn't work," he says. "The kids feel it. I did not like the idea of a divorce, and I thought maybe if we separated for a while, we could work things out. But after three months, except for the fact we both got lonely, there was no change in our attitudes. We weren't bitter with each other, although I felt some frustration. I thought maybe if we had gotten marriage counseling, we might have been able to work things out.

"Even though our decision to divorce was jointly made, I felt very rejected when she told me she didn't love me anymore. God, this really boggled me. I knew things weren't going well, but I didn't think it was that bad. She didn't want me to touch her, to be near her."

Carl's marriage ended because he and his wife agreed it had come to a dead end. They seemed to like each other, but their relationship could not sustain a marriage. This was also true for a clergyman-psychiatrist, who ended his second marriage through a joint decision. Gordon's first wife died after a very happy marriage, and a few years later he married again.

"We were very idealistic, and we had a family marriage ceremony where the kids were pronounced brothers and sisters and we were pronounced mother and father to our six children. I adopted her three children, and everyone was supportive of this idea.

"As is true in many second marriages, particularly if children are involved, the parents tend to be somewhat protective of their own children. My eldest daughter said she would never call my second wife 'Mother,' and I told her she didn't need to, but she had to call her something respectful, just as she would any adult. My two oldest called her by her first name, and my youngest called her 'Mom' by her own choice.

"For her part, Rosemary never really let me become a father to her children. Their first father had deserted the family for another woman, so she really didn't trust men, and I don't believe she trusted me. She didn't want her kids to get hurt again, so she wouldn't let me close to them, and when I was not around she would counter my requests to them. Toward the end of the marriage she told them they did not have to listen to me."

In addition to problems with the children, Gordon and his wife were also sexually incompatible. "It became apparent to both of us that our marriage was in trouble. We worked on our marital problems and the probability of divorce for three or four years.

Finally, I suggested that if we could ship her young son off to military school to give us a year to try to work things through, we might make it. But she would not agree to send her son away. Instead, she thought the best thing was a divorce, and I agreed.

"The break on the surface was so polite and so nice that I even helped her pack and move, and she helped me move into my new 'bachelor pad.' She even made the drapes for my bedroom."

Gordon said the divorce brought him relief because he and his wife had worked on it so long and very honestly. He also felt relaxed because he had lived so long with tension, staying out night after night to avoid going home. "I went back to my office, or to the bars and stayed there until I was sure she was asleep," he said. "When we happened to both be home, if she went to bed early I stayed up late; if she stayed up late, I went to bed early. We tried to avoid each other as much as we could for the last two years of our marriage.

"We put up a wonderful front, and I will give her credit. To my knowledge she has never downgraded me to her friends or even to her family. I still hear from her parents, and when I saw them recently we had a friendly time together. When the breakup came, it was not devastating to either of us."

Jack and Dianne decided jointly to end their marriage, too. They are a much younger couple, in their early thirties, with a seven-year-old daughter. He is a physician on a medical faculty at a large midwestern university. In retrospect, they realize they established their relationship and eventual marriage for the wrong reasons—a rebound situation after a divorce for both of them, plus a premarital pregnancy.

After graduation from medical school, Jack was told by his first wife that she no longer wanted the problems of being married to him while he struggled through an internship and residency. In addition, she had found someone else. At the same time, Dianne's first husband left her for a much younger woman. Jack and Dianne commiserated on their grief, their rejection, their hurt pride. When the young medical student had to go to another city for his internship, they decided to live together until both divorces were final. Then they would marry.

Jack says, "As we became more acquainted with each other, I began to doubt whether we were right for each other. Our backgrounds were very different, as were our values regarding many basic issues such as materialism. She was constantly reminding me of 'how rich we would be' when I finished my medical training and got into private practice. She had unrealistic dreams about how to spend all that money. This always has been a big bone of contention for us in that I have preferred a teaching position on our medical faculty instead of going into private practice. She constantly attacks my self-image as a person and as a professional because I am not pulling in $450,000 a year.

"She has a graduate degree in social work and supported us during our early relationship. Because of her financial support, she felt she had complete control of our lives. We bickered constantly. I was about to suggest we end our relationship when we discovered she was pregnant. We were married, and then began our years of discontent.

"She first asked me to leave when our daughter was fifteen months old, but instead we began counseling, trying to resolve our marital and personality difficulties. Five years down the road, we were still not enjoying being married. Oh, there were some good times when the money began rolling in, but it was never enough to suit her. Dianne also refused to socialize with members of the faculty and hospital staff. She said she felt socially inept, but I felt she could at least have made the attempt. Why did I endure this marriage? I felt I would do anything to keep our marriage together rather than to lose my daily contact with my beloved daughter."

Jack recalls that the tension in their home became so great and the fighting so traumatic that one day during a fight their daughter ran into her room screaming hysterically. Jack followed to comfort her. She told him she was going to run away so her parents would stop fighting.

"The next day Dianne and I agreed to see an attorney immediately to arrange for a no-fault divorce," Jack said. "The anguish suffered by our daughter made us both realize that a divorce would not possibly be as difficult for her as the hostility in our home. I moved out that next day—it was the day before Christmas, and I experienced the most lonely day of my life. But at least my little girl was free of the tension that was making her life so intolerable."

Even though the decision was made mutually, it was not without pain. Jack felt very much alone in his two-bedroom, sparsely furnished condo. His most compelling emotion was anger—anger for not having realized sooner the inevitability of divorce. He felt guilty for having helped subject his daughter to such distress while he and his ex-wife battled over every possible issue. He says, "I have the care of my daughter jointly, and I relish the sense of freedom from the stress of living in a household without love, affection, or intimacy between myself and my daughter's mother. My work and weekends with my daughter have alleviated any loneliness I felt early in my divorce process."

Men whose divorce was decided jointly often felt strong guilt feelings over the failure of their marriage, and like men whose wives divorced them, they felt rejected.

In most instances, the request to divorce comes as a shock to the spouse who is being asked for the divorce. This change is often unexpected and unwanted. Men whose wives tell them they are no longer loved, or that there is someone else, are shocked. Some feel their wives became more interested in their careers than in the marriages. Several men say their wives are dissatisfied with a poor sex life and no communication, and the couple just drifts apart. Many say their wives feel their children would be better off after a divorce than living in a hostile environment. Whatever the cause for the divorce, these men whose wives request it are devastated emotionally and physically for a considerable time, often as long as six months to a year.

On the other hand, men who initiate divorce, while suffering negative emotions primarily of anger and guilt, feel a keen sense of freedom. The most difficult obstacle for these men is how to tell their wives of the decision. They are afraid of the reaction and do not want to be hurtful, although they know they will be.

Phil, a forty-five-year-old businessman, says, "I needed months of counseling with a psychiatrist before I felt ready to tell her. When I finally told my wife I was leaving, I couldn't believe I could hurt her like I did. Yet, I couldn't understand why she didn't know that things were bad between us—over between us. I couldn't believe she preferred to finish her life out in the state of indifference that existed between us—where there was not love or interest in sex. Now, interestingly enough, after the divorce I see Mary as a different person—becoming a self-contained person. I see a much more confident lady. That old dependency pose is gone. She's a person who can do her own thing. She's going back to college to get her doctorate. Divorce has been good for both of us."

Daniel, a forty-year-old research botanist, feels divorce was a self-actualization process for him. "I grew up in the process of deciding what I really wanted out of life. After months of counseling with a therapist, I was prepared to tell my wife I wanted a divorce. I told her it was all my fault, that I took full responsibility for my decision. It was my decision to get single again. It wasn't that we didn't do things together, but there just was no sparkle in our lives. I expect life to sparkle for me, and if it doesn't, then I am unhappy. Actually, we didn't have much of a marriage. During the early part of our marriage she was going to college, and I am in a very high-pressured position which took most of my time getting established. We never have spent much time together. And besides, I was a tyrant—I was subject to mood changes, and it's a wonder she didn't want out before I suggested a divorce.

"Yet, she seemed very shocked, hurt at first, but in less than a year she was married again, so I think the trauma of divorce was not too great for her. I have been divorced for seventeen years, and am just beginning to contemplate remarriage. However, I seem to find contentment with my career and social life as a single person."

Regardless of the reasons, or which partner initiates the divorce, separation from a marriage is a psychologically painful experience for everyone in the family. We will learn in Chapter Two there is no ritual to help men through their grief, even when friends offer solace. They are in pain, but as men they are often unable to express their feelings. They find it difficult to believe their marriage is over. For some there is numbness, disbelief. For some, terrible anger, feelings of injustice. They feel physical pain along with emotional distress. They feel guilty for things they did or didn't do, said or didn't say. Divorce is a blow to their self-esteem. They have failed as husbands. They question their competence as human beings.

The aftermath of a divorce requires a grief process similar to that experienced after a wife's death. Following the divorce, the first step in mourning is to accept the reality of what has happened. Denial of the divorce leads to physical and emotional illness and even suicide attempts. After facing their anger and resentment, it is necessary for men to accept shared responsibility in the ending of the relationship, to forgive themselves and to let go of the bitterness and anger they feel toward their former wives.

Single-again men, whether divorced or widowed, must learn how to feel whole again. They must restore their sense of self-esteem. They must accept the fact that they have a deep emotional wound that will take time to heal.

The Widower

How the death of a spouse occurs influences the reactions and coping skills used to recover from the trauma. The reactions of men whose wives die suddenly or unexpectedly are very different from the reactions of those whose wives die after a lengthy illness.

Both categories of widowers express feelings of shock, denial, helplessness, loneliness, resentment, panic, self-pity, and confusion. They are depressed, sleepless, and unable to concentrate. Men whose wives die after an illness, however, express relief that the suffering is over. Some tell of their numbness and helplessness after the death and speak of an unbearable loneliness.

Men whose wives die after a sudden death express a more intense feeling of shock. Some are angry at themselves, wondering if they could have done something to prevent the death. They also express deep feelings of guilt and disbelief. There is very little difference between the two categories of widowers in the length of time taken to resolve their grief. Even after three years or longer in some cases, many of them still carry a residue of grief in their minds.

Death After a Lengthy Illness

Even when death comes after months of knowing the end is inevitable, few men are prepared for the emotions which arise. David was seventy-seven when his wife died of cancer after a six-month illness. "We knew she had an inoperable tumor, and I felt so helpless being a physician and not being able to do anything for my wife," he says tearfully. "At least she didn't suffer much. She stayed home until two days before her death, and her pain was adequately controlled with drugs. She was very comfortable, thank goodness. But I felt so helpless. Unable to do anything for her except to comfort her.

"The peculiar thing is, I think my helplessness made her feel I wasn't sympathetic with her condition. But if she only knew. She was conscious up to an hour before she died,and I was with her, holding her tenderly in my arms. I don't have any guilt about the relief I felt that her suffering was over, but I was angry, very angry over my inability to do anything for her. Near the end she would often say, 'Why don't you do something for me?' I suppose she thought there might be something else to do, but she was a nurse, and she knew as well as I did that nothing more could be done.

"Her death was so hard on me, knowing it was coming. I miss her so very much. I was a surgeon, and so often people have the impression that surgeons are unfeeling persons. This is not true. Some doctors may be, but I always suffered with my patients, perhaps more than I should have. But with my own dear wife my suffering was at times unbearable. I felt so alone and sad. I thought, given the news that my wife was going to die, that I would be prepared, but you are never prepared."

Charles, a sixty-year-old pastor, has also offered comfort to many grieving people, yet he, too, was unprepared for the emotions he felt when his wife died. He begins by saying, "This is going to be very difficult for me, and you will have to pardon my tears, because I can't talk about this without breaking down at some point. She had what we thought was a long-term cold. It would flare up and the doctor would give her some antibiotics. Then her cold would improve, and then back it would come.

"Eventually she began to tire more easily. We were avid skiers, and it got so she found it very difficult to breathe while skiing. At first, we just attributed this to her cold. As this pattern continued, she finally decided she should go into a large diagnostic center for a complete checkup. As I left her that evening resting comfortably in the hospital, I told her I would call her the next morning. I was feeling relieved that morning as I went over my papers in my office that soon we would know what her problem was and it could be alleviated.

"Then my phone rang. A tearful voice said to me, 'Honey, they just told me I have leukemia. Please come.' I felt as if an icicle had gone down my back, and I shivered all the way down my spine. I just sat in that chair, numb, feeling that cold chill. Then anger. Why couldn't they have waited until I returned to the clinic so that we could have heard the diagnosis together? Instead she had to call me. She was alone. Frightened.

"As I drove to the clinic, I told myself over and over that this couldn't be happening to her. They had made a mistake. But I finally awoke to the reality of our situation when a nurse said to me, 'I am so sorry your wife is terminal.' As reality hit me I again felt like someone had shot me full of ice water. This was January second and she died on March fourteenth.

"We had a good marriage—not without some disagreements, but I didn't have those feelings of guilt that so many persons who have lost a loved one seem to have. Anger, disbelief, loneliness, a terrible sense of being alone, these were my feelings. I was confused. I cried. My children and our many friends gave me the love and support I needed to make all the arrangements for her burial. I contacted a funeral director, and he carried out all the wishes that my wife had expressed before she died—the notice to the newspaper, the death certificate, a casket, the clothing she wanted to wear. Her decision had been made to have a closed casket at the wake and funeral service.

"The funeral service was held at our church, but I was unable to do the service, so grief-stricken was I. Then the services were over; we were at the grave site. Again even with all our family and friends around, I felt so alone; my loneliness overwhelmed me.

"Our children were all around for about a month, and we were able to go on a one-week vacation together the second month after her death in a small town in northern Minnesota where we had spent several vacations. So that took some of the edge off. When we returned and the children left, I felt sad and alone, but I knew I had to continue on with life. I started right in looking after things Marie had always done. I managed all right. But I would wake up in the middle of the night, and reach out for her, and she was not there. Then I was unable to go back to sleep again. I was able to cry in the privacy of our home, and this was a godsend, for it helped me get my feelings out in the open."

Men whose wives die after a terminal illness have an opportunity to begin their mourning process before the actual death, and to say their good-byes, but none are prepared for the pain they feel when the death actually occurs.

Unexpected Death

Men who suddenly lose their wives express more intense feelings of shock, anger, and deep-seated guilt than their counterparts whose wives die after an illness.

"Just fifteen minutes before I walked into our bedroom—when her lips were already purple—she had been watching the evening news with me," recounted Frank, a fifty-seven-year-old physician. "She hadn't been sick for even a day during our married life. It couldn't have happened! I wanted to try to resuscitate her, but I had to first call an ambulance. They were there in minutes, and those paramedics did everything possible to try to save her life. She was dead on arrival at the hospital. I was in a state of shock. There had been no inkling that something was wrong with her, yet she died of an acute heart infarction. She didn't have high blood pressure or any other signs of a heart condition.

"Disbelief. I just couldn't believe it had happened. Her death was so difficult for all of us. The Christmas tree was up with presents still under the tree and so were the birthday presents I had for her. I was so shocked and confused. And after the funeral, coming back and seeing her presents still under the tree—it was so difficult. I just broke down and sobbed, 'Why did it have to happen to my lovely wife?' I wouldn't allow myself to believe that she was actually dead. If it hadn't been for my wonderful son and daughter-in-law, I don't know how I would have survived. They just stood by me, gave me their support, and we got through it together."

When the shock of his wife's death began to subside, Frank felt anger, especially at himself. He still wondered if he could have done more for her had he gone into the bedroom sooner. "Down in my heart I don't think I could have done more," he said. "It was one of those acute situations that is over within five minutes. Yes, I was angry at myself. I also wondered if she had had problems prior to her death, and how come I didn't realize if something was wrong, being a doctor?"

"I often wonder how I coped during that first half-hour when they took her to the hospital. Deep down inside, I already knew she was dead, but it was still a great shock when that physician came out and told me she was gone.

"I was put under medication so that I could sleep. My friends were all so cooperative—offering me help and I took them up on their offers. I stayed with my son and his family for about three weeks after the funeral and playing with the grandchildren helped me pass the time. But then reality hit, and I knew I had to return to my home and work."

While Frank, a physician, experienced intense anger toward himself for failing to save his wife, he did receive sympathy and understanding from friends and acquaintances. This is in contrast to the negative attitudes toward men whose wives commit suicide. Their trauma of separation is compounded by societal attitudes of suspicion and avoidance. Is he to blame for his wife's suicide? Questions. Isolation from former friends. Even accusations by family members. These responses add to their own emotions of anger, shock, guilt, and postpone completion of the grief process for them.

Michael, forty-nine, whose wife committed suicide, says, "There were a lot of people who made nosey inquiries. I was really shut off by that, and I resented them. Concerned people are different. I have a couple of very good friends who tried to be very understanding, and I could talk to them. I remember Mary saying just what I needed to hear—'I know how terribly alone, how lost you must feel. I am so very, very sorry for you; can I cry with you?' I threw my arms around her, and we cried together for what seemed like hours. It was comforting being given permission to grieve, that it was all right to behave in whatever way I chose. But the questions asked by my wife's family, insinuating that I was to blame for my wife's suicide, tore me apart. I felt guilty enough without their adding to my guilt!"

William, fifty-one, whose wife, Betty, also committed suicide, felt a similarly deep-seated sense of guilt. "The shock of my wife's suicide was so great I needed immediate psychiatric help," he says, a deep frown covering his face at the memory. "She hanged herself in the garage, which was a terrible blow to me. She had climbed up on my tractor and fixed a rope on the beam and stepped off the tractor. We never had a car in that garage. That was my shop, and I had spent many, many happy hours puttering around in there. So I couldn't help but feel that in her last moments it was a blow directed at me. So at the moment I found her I felt anger—terrible anger. Why? The numbness I felt, the shock of death was completely immobilizing to me. This numbness, disbelief that she could do this, was with me for many days.

"Oh God, I felt hopelessly alone—a loneliness I had never experienced before. And the guilt! First the anger, and then the terrible guilt, as I felt I had let her down. I had not heeded the warnings that were right before me. Even those three days prior to her death she was crying constantly and saying she couldn't go on. And then on Sunday, the happiness and elation she had shown. That Sunday was a perfectly beautiful day for us. We went sailing, had a lovely day. But I should have known. She had many periods of depression and had even been hospitalized several times. She had a long record of depression, but also a long record of recovery. But the doctor had indicated she could be suicidal.

"So here was this feeling of guilt and the awful anger. I felt terrible resentment and anger toward her. I thought, 'goddamn it, you put me here in this psychiatrist's office.' I was emotionally drained. I felt nothing. Nothing. Things that were previously important to me were now unimportant. I had to reckon with my feelings of guilt before all this buried anger could come out."

William thinks men take on a tremendous responsibility toward their families, and when something like this happens, they can't help feeling responsible. "What didn't you do? What did you do? You have the feeling you let your wife down. That you haven't done your job," he said. "Will I ever overcome these terrible feelings of guilt? The pain of making the arrangements for her body to be taken away. The funeral. The thoughtless innuendoes, or maybe imagined, seemingly pointing a finger at me. Even my own daughter, who was particularly close to her mother, said some terrible things to me, blaming me for her mother's death as she let go of her anger. My two older children were very supportive of me. But I cried alone."

Grieving

It is never easy to let go. Adjustment to the death of a loved one requires a recognition of the reality of the loss, even though it feels impossible. The love these men had for their wives was deep and their grief intense. All widowers need help in living through their immediate period of grief to accept the death emotionally and intellectually. Many turn to their children for their primary support.

Even though he had deeper feelings of resentment about the tragic loss of his wife and mother of his children, men like John, who had very young children to care for, appear to cope better because they must mobilize. John's wife died of cancer after about a year's illness. He explains, "I think I was so confused with people running in and out and the funeral arrangements to make and all those things to do that I don't think I really did much thinking about how I felt. I was in a daze. Even when she died, I was in a daze. I had gone through many emotions while she was dying, but immediately after I wasn't feeling. We didn't have a wake, we had a funeral service and afterward our friends took us out to eat. It was only a few weeks later when my sister left and people began to withdraw from us, that I realized I was alone—totally alone. It seemed like such a huge burden all of a sudden thrust on me.

"What hit me most was the responsibility of caring for our four children, ages six through fifteen. My wife had played the nurturing role. Being a doctor, I was away from home a good deal of the time. It was an almost crushing blow realizing she was no longer here to help care for our children. I didn't know the first thing about managing a house. Everything seemed very black—all alone. I think I knew I would get over this feeling of helplessness. I had to, and soon. I must admit I did have feelings of bitterness at times being left with the problem of caring for my children and being so unprepared for this task.

"I missed my wife. But with my demanding work, my house and my children to look after, I didn't have time to get lonely. If I ever get lonely, all I have to do is look at the house, and I can find something to do. Children are certainly a problem, but they are also a lifesaver when it comes to being lonely. I count my blessings."

Grief, sorrow, guilt, anger, and self-pity are feelings bereaved people have to work through. They need help, and family and friends want to help; but even with support from others, grief is something one must really go through alone. Few understand the hurt unless they, too, have lost a loved one. Grief is not reasonable. It is emotional. Others cannot know what a man goes through unless he shares his pain, which is the significant problem facing men. Some are incapable of recognizing their true emotions, let alone revealing them to others. One must never assume a man is not suffering intense grief just because he is not showing it.

"I cry, but I cry in private. No one really knows how deeply I hurt," says Gordon, fifty-four, who lost his wife to cancer just two weeks after her illness was diagnosed. "I was angry. I could not believe she had died. All our plans and dreams for the future—shot right down the drain. Even after four years, I still find myself asking God why He had to take her. Maybe if I could have cried it would have helped me get rid of my feelings. But I don't cry easily. And I don't understand others' crying. I consider myself tough. When my wife cried, I would start laughing at her. I cried just a little at my wife's funeral. I felt so choked up I thought I was going to die. My son couldn't cry either. At the wake, he said, 'You know, here is my mother and your wife lying here dead, and it is a big loss to us. Yet we have to be a strong pillar of support for all the people who have come to honor her. And we can't cry. We have to be strong and we are. Friends can put their heads on our shoulder and they cry—but we aren't allowed to do this.' I can remember some women telling me how they admired me at the wake and funeral—so brave—just like a man who is in complete control of himself. How little they knew!"

It is important to grieve openly, and widowers who are able to get their feelings out find adjustment to life without their wives comes more quickly. To deny or ignore one's grief delays a return to normal living. Terry, a thirty-year-old widower, was afraid to show his feelings. He had a "macho image" to preserve. His wife of just six months was killed by a drunken driver. A month later he tried to commit suicide. "I was always taught that real men don't cry—that even when you hurt, you pretend all is right. You can't be afraid of anything. I could not show my feelings—my fears. Anger I could express, but not my pain." Terry's pent-up feelings came out in a self-destructive act. He had suffered great physical distress, such as sleeplessness, lack of appetite and migraines. To reach acceptance, Terry turned to a professional for help after his suicide attempt.

It is clear there are often dramatic differences in the way widowed and divorced men describe their marriages. Divorced men report primarily negative aspects of the marriage. They are unable to communicate about their marital concerns and feel little compatibility with their wives, although many had not contemplated divorce. They were willing to "tough it out." Widowers, on the other hand, generally describe their marriages positively.

The reactions of men whose wives initiate divorce are similar to those of widowers—shock, disbelief, panic, anger, resentment, despair, and self-pity. They became depressed, sleepless, and unable to concentrate.

Men whose wives die suddenly experience guilt and anger, as do men who initiate divorce, but for different reasons. These men are angry at themselves and feel guilty they did not do more to prevent the death. Men who initiate divorce are angry at themselves because they took so long to take the first step. Their guilt is over possible hurt to their children as a result of their actions or non-actions. All feel initially lonely in their lives as single-again men.

2

Coming to Terms with the Loss

In the first months following the death of a wife, most widowers find life almost unbearable. They are plagued by loneliness and self-doubt. Did they do everything possible to prevent her death?

Yet widowers may be the more fortunate of the two types of newly single men because there are established rituals to help with the early stages of their loss. Divorced men have no such rituals—they find themselves truly alone.

Both types of newly single men, however, experience similar physical symptoms, including lack of appetite, sleeplessness and stomach distress.

Similar, too, are the coping mechanisms used by divorcing men and widowers to overcome their grief. Some join support groups and find new friends. Family members and close friends are sympathetic listeners. Some develop new hobbies. Some submerge themselves in work. Some seek professional help, while others may prefer to "tough it out." Divorced men seem more prone to increase their drinking. Both types of newly single men find they need to work through many feelings before they can accept and adjust to the reality of what has happened to their marriages and begin to enjoy life again.

The Divorced Man

Basic to overcoming grief is the acceptance of reality. Grief is a process the divorced man, as well as the widower, must experience.

It is always lonely. No one else can go through it for him. He has to rid himself of the empty feeling—the feeling of numbness he develops to protect himself from feeling too much pain. He may feel as though everything is unreal, and that he is out of control. Suicide feelings are common. Many divorced men say they went a little crazy during the first stages of the divorce process.

If a man is to regain his sense of reality—that his marriage has ended—he must stop denying the fact and allow himself to be angry over what has happened. He will be angry at himself and angry at his wife. He may wish to re-establish his marriage, but it is best to let go, for to hang on to a dead relationship causes him to feel as though life has no purpose. He feels depressed. He thinks about all he worked for, all that happened during his marriage, and how his efforts were for naught. But one day he will begin to accept what has happened to his marriage; he will be able to let go of the past—to find relief from his grief and to enjoy his freedom.

Men Who Are Left

Divorced/divorcing persons are at great risk for psychiatric disorders, accidents, and disease. Thus, strategies for coping successfully with divorce are important. Clinicians believe that, if handled properly, the divorce process can lead to a new sense of self-worth, development of better relationships, and freedom to accomplish important new goals.

The key variable related to divorce adjustment is who wanted the divorce. Men whose wives initiate divorce find it more difficult to adjust, and adjustment takes longer. Ernest expressed his feelings through writing and talking. He was an Air Force pilot, age thirty, when his wife told him she no longer loved him. "I was still in love with her, and things were very painful for me—the rejection, the anger, denial, and loneliness. It took me over six months to get in a shape where I could even meet people. It took me even longer to realize I wasn't the incompetent, unlovable, worthless bum she had labeled me."

Ernest's main problem was that he didn't have anybody to talk to, being in the armed services and miles away from the only friends he had. So he wrote hundreds of letters to his wife, getting his feelings out on paper, but he never mailed them.

Finally, Ernest realized he could not handle the heartache, the actual physical pain he was feeling, and got into a group that talked about problems common to divorced people. "We became good friends, and it takes friendship to get over this painful experience," he says. "I learned to understand that my relationship with the woman I still loved had ended. She no longer loved me. She had remarried. You have to get out and become involved in other interests to get your mind off your own problems. You can't do it by yourself. You have to let other people show you that you are an okay person so you don't continue to wonder what kind of person you really are. I always thought I was too strong to cry, but I sure learned quickly from my group that it was okay to cry."

Gary, a forty-nine-year-old college professor, also found group support helpful. "I cried when I was alone, and the head of my department was very sympathetic. I spent several hours in his office every week, and he just listened to me and let me get my feelings out. He didn't offer advice—just listened. Then I began going to group meetings where I found people going through the same things as I was. It was also good to meet people farther along the line to recovery who could say to me, 'Hey, no matter how bad it seems now, things will get better.' "

Gary also found that keeping busy helped keep his mind off his hurt feelings. For the first six months he felt a great deal of stress—waking up at three in the morning, unable to sleep, having difficulty concentrating during the day. His usually high energy level was very low, and he couldn't do any work on his research even though he was close to his contract deadlines. Gary finally managed to gain control again by trying to take things one day at a time, by restoring routine and structure to his life. He shopped, bought furniture for his apartment, and began to work on his research. He really started again from scratch. "It's important to remember that the feelings and pain are natural," Gary says. "If you weren't feeling pain, there would be something wrong with you. We all have to go through this mourning process—to work it through. No one can do it for you.

"If your wife initiates the divorce, you feel a terrible sense of rejection, but as time goes on I have become more distant from her and the pain is less. I am letting go. It's almost the same thing that happens when a child grows up and leaves home—the distancing that takes place."

Charles, a professor, age forty-eight, is letting time heal him and has come to accept being alone. Alone for nine years, he has yet to remarry. At the time of the split he moved into a small apartment, which was confining after living in a large home with all its conveniences. He missed his children, he missed everything. He thought it would help if he changed jobs and so moved to another state, but he did not know anyone there and was very lonely.

"Eventually I realized I would not help myself by just sitting around, so I went out and met new people. I didn't wait around for someone else to fill the void in my life," he recalls. "I just gradually worked out my frustrations. The greatest one was having to be without my children. To me, the best part of being married was having the children. I don't want to exaggerate, but I think I did pretty well as a father, if not so well as a husband."

For several years Charles lived in a one-room efficiency apartment where, after rent, food, and phone were paid, he had only thirty dollars a month left for other things. There was little he could do except use the university library and other free facilities, which he enjoyed. He remembers going to the library, meeting other faculty and having good conversations. "I remember wondering what would happen to me if I were a blue-collar worker with nothing to do but go to a bar to drown my sorrows with drink," he recalls. "I just felt, 'Gee, now is the time to read all this stuff I always wanted to read.'"

"I still haven't learned to cook, but so what? I'll eat garbage for the rest of my life, to not be in another messy marriage. Living by myself was not too difficult after I made up my mind that my marriage was over. I gradually picked up certain skills for keeping house. Now things are so much better for me than they were nine years ago that the petty frustrations and annoyances that come along for a single person seem a small price to pay for the peace and freedom I feel. I have learned to enjoy myself as a person."

Men Who Initiate Divorce

The emotions mentioned most frequently by men who initiate divorce are loneliness, guilt, and anger. What do these men do to alleviate their feelings?

Kent, a forty-two-year-old professor still single after fifteen years, began his divorce because, he says, his wife cheated, lied, and was completely irresponsible. They had no children. "I was happy to be free of this bad marriage, but still there were periods of being lonely. I joined a support group of people with something in common—divorce. I enjoyed the social aspects of this group very much, having a few drinks with them, 'happy-hour' on Fridays, picnics, dinners, and parties. I increased my exercise, played golf more frequently, joined a gourmet dinner club and generally have enjoyed being single."

Mike, a psychologist, age thirty-eight, has been divorced for six months. He divorced his wife after sixteen years of marriage because living with her became impossible. "I finally became angry enough to leave a very exasperating situation. I have had a lot of things thrown at me—plates, dishes, vases, and she came after me with a knife one day—and this was in front of our children. Right before our separation I became so angry at her I told her I could wipe her out any time I wanted to. I had to hold her right down on the floor to quiet her down, and the kids saw that, too.

"To our friends, I am the 'bad guy,' and goddamn it, I am angry about that. I might have been better off bullying her all through our marriage because I think she actually expected that. She needed someone to knock her around like her parents did, I guess. But I surely did not want to live that way. And it was not good for the children."

Mike was also angry about their finances. His wife kept the house, and he moved into a condo. It was a financially taxing period because she expected him to absorb all the costs of the house plus his own expenses. She worked during most of the marriage but quit her job since the divorce. Mike thinks this is an excuse—that she must "suddenly" devote all of her time to their two sons, ages nine and seven. Despite this, Mike knows he did the right thing.

"Aside from anger at my wife and guilt because of the children, I enjoyed wonderful freedom and peace after the separation," Mike said. "I realized our friends were uncomfortable about taking sides, so that meant going out and making new friends. It took me a long time to make friends in the first place, but I did, and I am happy with my new life. Lack of friends is the most devastating part of being separated." Mike joined clubs, single-parent groups and singles groups where he met people he could talk to and have fun with.

"You have to try to meet a lot of people, but you should keep a good reign on your emotions or you will find yourself getting close to people, which can be a trap," he says. "You have to keep a bit of distance from new people in your life. That may be hard to do, for some people are very charming, but they can be very exploitive at the time in your life when you are very vulnerable."

Mike says the most helpful thing for him is to realize he is not going to solve all his problems at once, or all by himself. He knows, too, that he can wait and look at his problems from a distance. He especially does not want to rush into any new relationships, fearing he may get into something just as bad as before, or worse.

Don, a physician, age forty, has been divorced about ten months. He offers some good advice on how to cope with a divorce that has been initiated by the man. First, he talks briefly about his marriage, to lend perspective to why he wanted out. "I was going with Sally for about six months when we discovered she was pregnant. So I played the 'good guy' and married her. I was under the illusion—like a lot of people—that our marriage would automatically work. I cared for her, but I did not love her. I think that's the thing that finally hit me seventeen years later. And I did not want to continue to live in a relationship the rest of my life that could bring me no pleasure. I realized I had never had a chance in my life to feel independent, to feel free to make my own choices."

Don says he jumped from one dependent relationship into another. His parents put him through medical school, and when Sally got pregnant, they were married in his first semester of medical school. To save money, Sally moved in with her parents, but just as Don entered his internship and they could afford to be together, he was drafted into the service during the Vietnam War. So it was almost nine years before they really settled down into a 'normal' marriage.

"Life was meaningless and dull for me. Sally and I lived more as brother and sister than as husband and wife. I take a good share of the blame for the deterioration of our relationship. As a physician, I always put my work first and my family second. There were times when I would want sex, and she was never ready. We would go weeks, months without sexual intercourse. But still we could never find a common ground on which to discuss the problems we had.

"Then all of a sudden I experienced love for the first time in my life. It began with a really nonsexual intimate relationship with someone I worked closely with. I began to fantasize how it would be like married to her, and I knew I wanted out of a dull, dead marriage.

"It took me six months or more of therapy to get to the decision that I must get a divorce, and then all of a sudden one day I woke up at 6:00 A.M., got up, and made up my mind that I was going to do it. Things had been continuing to deteriorate, and it was time to put a stop to it. It took additional therapy to tell Sally of my decision. She, of course, was willing to just stick it out with the way it was. What really surprised me was how shocked she was when I told her I was going to leave. She wouldn't believe it. Yet there were so many signs of our deteriorating relationship that even some of our close friends remarked that they were not surprised at the divorce."

After the divorce Don lived in a dream world. He felt good, more relaxed than he had in years. He says he had almost a born-again Christian feeling, in touch with reality for the first time in his life. He had the freedom to be himself.

Yet Don was ignoring his feelings—working long hours, drinking more, running three to five miles a day. He even tried marijuana once and had what he calls a "whangbang" sexual affair that lasted only a few weeks. "It's so damn important to find professional help to understand your feelings," he says, thinking back. "I think the reason why so many blue-collar workers have such great difficulty coping with their grief is their lack of resources. They have a macho image to preserve, and can't admit to themselves their need for professional help, nor can many of them afford it. We all have emotions that need to be expressed. I feel sorry for those guys who are unable to talk with anyone about their feelings except perhaps a bartender over some beers.

"I was really down before I sought professional help. I even contemplated suicide. I had such psychological pain, so intense that I couldn't stand it. I know what a guy feels like when he decides to kill himself—you end the psychological pain. I have talked to a lot of my friends who have contemplated suicide once or twice in their lives, so this is not an unusual way of escape in our society.

"My psychiatrist told me this was not unusual for the male. What we do is to suppress our feelings and push them down so deep we feel we're in a vacuum. I had a deep-seated distrust of people. I went through a real cynical stage trying to determine if I was morally right in leaving my wife. I developed an ulcer. So I had to work hard with my therapist trying to get inside myself and feel the feelings that I had, trying to explain my mode of actions, especially when I found out that Sally was so blown away by my leaving."

Don's advice to others in his situation: Join a support group or seek professional help. He says although a therapist may not be able to cure the problems, at least he or she can point out where the problems are. Therapy helped Don stop demanding too much from himself and learn to let go. "You need to listen to your own feelings, listen to your gut feelings and believe them," he says. "For a long time I didn't really want to believe my gut feelings, but I do now. I am letting go, I am making new friends, and I am living in the now, the reality of today.

"You also have to come to grips with the fact that you are not going to be able to solve all of your problems and understand all of your feelings—some of these emotions and problems may be with you for the rest of your life. And I still think that talking out our feelings, coming to grips with them, helps you cut the ties with the past. Talk. Talk. Talk. I wish now I had been able to get into some kind of divorce group but at the time I felt that I was 'above that' as a professional person. I really believe group therapy would have been as important as individual therapy. Groups help you make new friends, keep you from the tendency to withdraw from contact with others."

It is clear that a man who initiates his divorce has difficulty coping with his feelings, as does the man whose wife initiates the divorce. Anger, self-doubt and guilt are as difficult to cope with, as are feelings of rejection, worthlessness, disbelief, and denial. Divorced people need the support of family and friends during the entire divorce process. Adjustment may be hastened and stress lowered through interaction with sympathetic people who will just listen to the outpouring of emotions felt by the divorced/divorcing person.

A Joint Decision to Divorce

Divorce is never easy, even for those who have mutually decided upon it. Gordon, the sixty-year-old minister-psychiatrist, says even though he was embarrassed, as a professional in his field, to admit to the world he had failed at marriage, and even though he found it difficult to explain to his friends and colleagues what had happened, at least he did not have guilt, and he did not come out as the 'bad egg' or the 'poor rejected soul,' as many divorced men do. He says his children, colleagues and close friends were very supportive of him, and he was seldom lonely. Everyone knew their divorce was a joint decision, and it was civilized, except for the monetary provisions, where Gordon played the role of gentleman. He now feels he was "taken to the cleaners."

Nonetheless, Gordon's philosophy is, "No matter what happens, it has certain possibilities for something that would never have happened otherwise. When something bad happens, I say, 'Now what can I make good out of this?'

"To people who say, 'I'm divorced, poor me,' I say, 'Poor you, heck; now is the time to start again. Darn few of us get new chances in life. And you know a lot more when you get a new chance than you did in your previous chance.' I didn't want to be widowed. I didn't want to be divorced, but I have learned something that can allow me to better understand the feelings of somebody else who has lost a relationship. So the best advice I can give about coping with divorce, or any other problem one has, is to make the most of any situation you are in. Get out and circulate. Keep busy. Find a good friend, family member—someone to whom you can ventilate your emotions. Life goes on."

Jack, the young physician, says he was very lonely away from his home and young daughter, but he expected that. Otherwise, he enjoyed his freedom from the tension that had pervaded his home life. He says, "I am a private person and do not bring my personal life into my work world, so I shared my feelings with no one except my mother. She happens to be a family counselor, and right after my divorce she came for a visit. I was able to talk out my feelings, my resentment, my anger about what had happened and I felt much better."

Jack says he spends even more time now with his work, exercises more than he did before and generally takes very good care of his health, which he thinks is important. "Some guys after a divorce live on junk food and booze," he says. "It is as necessary to take good care of your body as it is your mind. In times of stress, physical impairments can take hold unless your body is also well cared for. After six months I am quite well adjusted and very happy with my life as a single person."

Carl, an electrician, found that group support was very important in giving him a sense of direction. "I have joined three different groups. The best one is a small rap group where we get together and really share our feelings. The large group provides a good chance for socializing. Our decision to divorce was so mutual that I have no hang-ups. No guilt. Very little anger. I am never lonesome because I can see my children any time I want, and my ex-wife and I are still good friends."

Men whose divorces are decided upon jointly seem to adjust rather quickly and with few problems to single life. They have little guilt and anger is minimal. They certainly do not feel the worthlessness that is so difficult to handle by the man whose wife initiates the divorce. Generally, joint decisions to divorce leave fewer scars, relative to the number suffered by men in other types of divorce. These men seem to be able to accept their new roles and are able to break away from the former marriage more readily than men in other circumstances.

The Widower

With family and friends around, funeral arrangements to be made, perhaps a sedative, a few extra highballs, a widower might feel he is handling the situation well. But usually there comes a moment when he realizes he is alone. He misses so much from the relationship he had with his wife. The memories of their love, the happy moments, the birth of their children, the ups and downs, the decisions they shared together—and now everything is changed.

"The first few months after my wife's death were almost unbearable—the loneliness, the emptiness," is a typical statement made by men who have lost a wife. Thomas found that no one outside his immediate family wanted to talk to him about his wife's death. He says, "Their attitude seemed to be that I had buried Terry on Friday, was back to work the following week and on Saturday I would be out looking for a date. There seemed to be little empathy for me—they acted at work as though my wife never had existed."

Thomas says the reality of that attitude became painfully clear when people stopped helping. The first month their friends brought supper over every night, offered to baby-sit, called to check on his well-being. Suddenly that all stopped. Thomas had to carry the whole burden of his grief himself. "Lots of crazy things would go through my mind, like how was I ever going to get over the loneliness," he says. "I woke up in the morning and the other side of the bed was still perfectly smooth, and I would realize again she wasn't there, and the emptiness was very depressing."

Whether a wife dies suddenly or after a lingering illness, the pain is there and the widower must work through his feelings alone. No one can do this for him. The important difference between a sudden death and a terminal illness is the shock of the unexpected death, with no opportunity to "mend fences" or to prepare in any way for the end.

Charles' wife died after an illness. Before her death, he says, "All the barriers to communication had disappeared, and we talked about everything. I was grateful for that." And David says, "I didn't feel any guilt for the relief I felt that her suffering was over." These two felt anger, disbelief, and the terrible sense of being alone, but they did not experience the shock that Bob did when his wife died after what had been considered a successful operation. "We were all ecstatic with the news that the tumor was not malignant and then, suddenly during the night, she died. The shock and disbelief were so great I cannot tell you what it was like for us. I was filled with a deep-seated anger. I blamed the nurses, the doctors, God. Until I was able to get my anger out, I found no solace for my grief. My belief in God finally gave me a way to accept what had happened."

Guilt, anger, and self-pity must be vented before one can find inner peace. Guilt is probably the most difficult emotion to cope with because few people take the time to demonstrate their love to those close to them, never thinking that tomorrow they may not have the opportunity. They don't say the things they feel in their hearts. Then when a loved one dies, they are left with thoughts of, "Why didn't I? Why didn't I get her to the doctor sooner? Why didn't I pay attention to her symptoms? Why didn't I tell her I loved her more often?"

But life goes on. And pain begins to subside as the bereaved recognize their reactions and emotions and work through them.

Many factors influence the ability of the bereaved to cope with their losses, including the type of death, the degree of the widower's emotions, personal philosophies about life and death, and the presence of children. Age, too, is a factor and it seems only natural that the longer two people have been married, the more difficult it is to adjust to living alone. Each widower copes with his grief differently.

Richard, an office manager, age sixty-three, whose wife died of a stroke, has recovered beautifully primarily because of his philosophy toward life. "Even after four years," he told me, "I miss her every day, but I understand what happened and my reactions. The pain is not so poignant now. I feel if she had to go, this was the best way for her to die—suddenly, and without prolonged suffering. And I know she would not have been happy had she survived to be a helpless vegetable."

Richard said the first thing he did was let it all out. He often got up in the middle of the night and paced around, talking to himself and sometimes to his cat. If he felt like crying, he did. He faced the reality of her death. "I admitted to myself that it happened. There are some people who just refuse to accept the situation and bang their heads against the wall screaming, 'Why me?' I realized that human beings have been dying since the creation of man, and it's always happening to someone somewhere. I felt I wasn't singled out for any particular punishment—so I didn't have to wallow in self-pity or to feel guilty. We had a good married life, and we loved each other. We expressed our love frequently, so I didn't have any regrets that way—and I knew she was better off dead than living a lingering death. I made up my mind that sooner or later I had to make a life for myself, too."

Richard believes widowers have an inclination to idealize, to put the dead person on a pedestal. He realized within a short time that he and his wife were like everybody else. They had their faults, but they did have a good married life. "I'm just very happy that I've had her for thirty-five years," he said. "It took me a while to finally see some good in this thing. But I have thanked God for all the time we spent together—the things that we had learned together, the times we had together. I could look back with a certain degree of satisfaction at our life together."

Richard said the biggest problem he had to deal with was being alone. At first he called it loneliness and then it began to change to "I'm alone but I'm not necessarily lonely." He has a comfortable home and enjoys being by himself, coming and going as he pleases. "If I'm tired, I go to bed, and if I want to get up I do. If I want to have a meal at three in the afternoon I have one. And if I decide to stay in the office or do something downtown, I do," he says. "I am enjoying my independence, and I am not lonely. There are times when I think, 'Oh my God—nobody here but me and the cat.' But then I get busy with something and being alone is no problem."

Richard finds his work has a stabilizing effect, and he isn't sure he would be able to face a whole day of disorganization with nothing demanding. He keeps himself healthy through running and other exercise, and takes classes in nutrition and cooking. "All in all, I have made a good transition from a beautiful marriage to single blessedness," he concluded.

Richard's own philosophy toward life and death, his relative freedom from guilt and anger, the loving support of his children, and a deep and abiding love for his dead wife all help him cope without professional or outside help.

William, however, whose wife committed suicide, had a more difficult time and was unable to make this adjustment without the aid of a psychiatrist. At age fifty-one, William experienced classic symptoms of depression. He felt dejected, lost interest in his business, and was unable to concentrate. His physical symptoms included lack of appetite, sleeplessness, and stomach distress, and his emotions went from extreme elation to deep inertia. He lost interest in his physical appearance and felt completely out of control of his life.

Wisely, William sought professional help. The psychiatrist prescribed antidepressant drugs along with therapy, and helped William recognize his deep-seated guilt and anger.

William finally managed to get control of his emotions so that he could cope with his grief. His advice for others: "I would tell a person to believe that things will get better, but it takes time. No one can rid you of your grief. You have to work it out, and I think seeking help from a professional counselor or attending self-help groups helps you work through your emotional pain. There is no timetable that will suit everybody. Each man is unique, and each man has had a different experience and a different relationship."

William says he was not a good candidate for dealing with loss. He had lost his parents through divorce, and because when he was a child other family members were frequently ill, he often was

shipped off to faraway relatives. In addition to his fear of abandonment, his sister died, his mother was put in an institution, and both
his father and wife committed suicide. "I have always enjoyed being
around people. I enjoy the people I work with. I enjoyed the
presence of Betty," William said. "And, then suddenly it was all torn
away. She was dead. God, I went through hell trying to think of
myself as a 'me' instead of a 'we.'

"I drove myself into going back to work, into seeing people and
joining groups. What really jarred me back to my senses was a crisis
in my business. When I realized I would lose my business, I became
realistic about my life and began to concentrate on living." Although
William definitely needed professional help, in the end, it was his
own determination to get on with living that saved him.

Charles, a sixty-year-old pastor, did not feel guilty, but he
suffered from terrible sadness and loneliness. He found an important
therapeutic release—he poured out his feelings in a journal as if he
were writing to his wife. He says he told her things he would have
said if she were still alive, very intimate things:

> Marie, my darling, I want you so badly, to feel your softness against
> my body, to caress you, to hold you closely. I miss the warmth of
> your tender kiss as I awaken in the morning. I feel so sad and lonely.
>
> We have lots to be happy for. You know, even our fights were
> good because after a few shouts, we would just laugh and that would
> be the end of it. We had a good marriage, and I have been so sad that
> our happiness has ended so abruptly. We shared sadness as well as
> joy. I can remember so well when our first child was stillborn, and we
> were stationed far away from home during the war. But this loss
> brought us even closer, and we joined our tears in grief. I never told
> you then how brave I thought you were. I know you held back some
> of your feelings for my sake.
>
> When each of our four children was born, I felt an even greater
> love for you, but I understood your lack of desire for sex. I hope I
> never required you to have me when you didn't want to. I have an
> intense sex drive, but I took care of it by masturbating. You know,
> honey, if I don't have an ejaculation within ten days, I get involuntary
> emissions that can be hopelessly embarrassing. I once had an emission
> while I was preaching a sermon, and that made me realize I just
> couldn't be celibate between times when you felt the desire for sex.
>
> We have had many beautiful, loving sexual experiences. I have

never desired another woman—you have been my whole life. Now that you are gone, it feels like more than half of my life has been cut off. All of a sudden there is a whole big chunk taken out of my life—and that emptiness.

I know you told me that someday I would find another woman to love and to grow with. But right now I can't imagine that. Oh, Marie, I am crying and cannot see what I am writing.

Charles explains he never felt his dead wife knew what he was writing, nor that she might answer him. "If there is anything at all after this life, I don't have any sense of making contact with people we loved in this life," he said. "At any rate, I did find myself calling her name out of the pure sadness that I converse with her. The writing was not so much conversing as saying what I felt, things I would like to say to her if she were alive."

Charles said what probably helped him the most was his ability to cry, along with his writing. It felt good each time he wrote down his feelings, and he felt no strangeness about doing it. Nor did he have a sense of loss after three months when he stopped writing because his regular vocation started again and he had no more inclination to write.

Another good coping mechanism is simply to talk about the loss. Thomas, twenty-nine, whose wife was killed in an auto accident, says, "First and of greatest importance is to talk about your wife's death to as many people as will listen to you—even if you have to drag them off into a corner. You just have to talk. People are not going to ask you about your feelings. They seem to think you have no feelings because you are a man. Your friends think they can't bring up your loss because it's too painful for them, and so they will talk about the weather and the baseball game. I've had to force the issue to get people to talk with me about Terry's death—especially during the first two months."

Thomas also advises physical self-care. "Take care of your health," he says. "Get as much exercise as you can. I ran in the morning so that I was very physically tired, and it was enough to relax me. I had very good thoughts during the time I was running that first summer after Terry died. I would almost go into a state of meditation. Mentally, it was the best thing I ever did for myself along with getting enough sleep and eating the right food. And above all, lay off the booze—alcohol will only tear down everything you are trying to build up."

He concludes, "If you have children, do everything in your power to let them know you love them. Your children in turn can give you strength. They motivated me to go on with my living."

Whatever other ways they use to cope, most widowers say it is most important to recognize that grieving takes time. David, who was married for fifty years, said the fact that he and Virginia had a very happy marriage and lots of love gave him pleasant memories, and his children and grandchildren were a great comfort. "But," he says, "my friends seem to be dropping away. I don't get invited out like we used to be as a couple. You are an odd person in the group. My friends just don't like to think about death.

"The first thing for a widower to remember is that grieving takes time. You can't push it. When you are ready to go out, you will feel it. I am very happy mourning for my wife for a while. It may seem like a contradiction, 'being happy to mourn,' but it isn't. We had a long, happy life, and it is right that I mourn. I have fond memories that are important and comforting to me. My loneliness after a happy marriage is very painful. The transition from being married to being alone is very difficult even after six months. I still forget that she is gone. Imagination is a powerful thing."

Life does go on for these men. They cope with their grief, but for each man the length of that road to recovery is different. Seeking professional help, accepting the death, expressing feelings through crying or talking or writing, plunging into work and other activities are some of the ways widowers cope. They recover from grief when they recognize their emotions and find ways to work through them. The road to recovery from grief may be hastened by listening to the advice of those who already have traveled that road. The knowledge that they will recover from a loss gives many widowers hope that happiness will be forthcoming.

Being with others who need and love us brings a comforting sense of security and closeness. But there comes a day when everyone seems to return to the patterns of daily life, and the widower finds himself left to his own devices for coping. He has to establish a new identity as a single person.

Some, such as Sam, a fifty-year-old dentist, find it extremely difficult to accept their single state. "I felt a sense of rootlessness. My wife had always taken care of everything for me. I knew that it was no longer 'we' but how does one let go of the past? My whole sense of who I am is tied to my wife. It is difficult adjusting to this new identity. I did many crazy things that first year after my wife's death. I spent money like wild and then I would say, 'Why did I buy that?' I bought an exercise bike although I knew I would never use anything like that—and I am usually quite tight with money.

"Even now, after four years, I often still think of myself as a 'we.' I am beginning to change many things in the house, even though during the first years the sameness gave me pleasure. I am gradually packing her things away and replacing them with items of my choice. My home is now decorated in a more 'masculine' manner. I am still going through the transition to being a single man. But I feel contented.

"I got hold of myself, as I tell my patients to do, and became involved in living. I was fortunate that I have a good occupation which I like, and I could get back to work which left me little time to think about my problems. In addition to relationships with new friends, I returned to other activities, such as golf and going to my health club for swimming. It is good to find a number of things that one enjoys doing so that whenever you feel anxious, you can find something to busy yourself with."

It is through involvement with life that many widowers are able to let go of their grief. Jim, for example, when told to get a new hobby, took up dancing lessons. Then he became a member of a weekly dancing club and has literally danced his way out of his depression. As he says, "I have met many other persons in the same boat, and that is comforting. And I have met many interesting ladies. In fact, the girl I am engaged to was a lovely lady I met at these dances."

Sam says, "I continued entertaining friends for dinner just as my wife and I did. I took courses in gourmet cooking, and now my friends look forward to an invitation from me. On New Year's Eve, I invite a group of twelve friends over, and I love playing host. I guess I am no different from most widowers I have talked to, in that I have been unable to keep up relationships with previous married friends. Most of my new friends are couples living in my townhouse complex who are young and with children. I have become an extra grandpa for them. I remember their birthdays and take the children little presents. I take groups to the zoo on weekends, and I am always being invited in by these young couples for cocktails or a meal. You can't expect others to arrange your social life. You have to get involved and take your social life into your own hands as you establish your identity as a single person."

In the early stages of grief, counseling is often needed. Referrals for grief counseling services may be obtained through one's religious affiliation, through mental health associations and through public health departments. Self-help groups are sponsored nationally and locally by various church and community groups. A phone call to a public office or a look in the yellow pages of the phone book will provide information about community services and organizations that are available to formerly married persons.

A rabbi talks about what solace he was able to give a grieving young mother who had lost an eighteen-month-old son. "I asked her," he says, "if she would have wanted to miss the happiness of those eighteen months with her son in order to be spared the pain of losing him. The young mother thanked God for those few months of happiness." Love is seldom without pain, for when we love, we always run the risk of losing that love. It is a risk worth taking. The knowledge that we will recover gives us hope that we will once again find love and happiness. With this hope, we can regain our self-confidence. We can go on alone.

Helping our children go on, however, can be more of a challenge. Regardless of how the decision to divorce is reached, most children suffer in some way when a family breaks up. And regardless of how well a widower works through his own feelings of grief, he may have difficulty helping his children face the reality of death and cope with their own sense of loss. In our next chapter we look at the relationships between newly single men and their children, as fathers and children move through the period of transition and begin to adjust to their new lives.

3

How Losing a Parent
Affects the Children

THE loss of a loved one is difficult at any age, but it is particularly painful for children. The degree of emotional investment and dependence of a child upon a parent is far greater than that of any other relationship a child may experience.

The most common cause of parental absence today is divorce. The absent parent is usually intermittently available to the child, yet occasional accessibility is not altogether satisfactory. In death, the loss is permanent. Although it may be overwhelming to the child or difficult to accept because of mixed feelings about the dead parent, death is final and the details do not change. Death, unlike divorce, does not require constant adaptation and adjustment.

Parental absence for any reason may be perceived as a loss of security, nurturing, and affection—a loss of essential emotional support upon which the child formerly relied. Children lose their identity as a member of a two-parent family as well as daily interaction with the absent parent. Because of these psychological stresses, the children typically feel depressed and anxious, and tend to deny what is happening. We may not be aware of the depth of anguish they harbor, the pain, the anger, the sadness. Ron, eighteen, wrote this poem explaining how he felt about the death of his mother:

> *If only I could have said goodbye*
> *If only I could have hugged her*
> *She would have known I was there and always*

would be.
The coldness and the vacant stare consumed me into
the world of dense wilderness.
The path out is so hard to find. The leaves wind
around my head as if to strangle the life
out of me.
I shall escape.
And when I do, I'll be one step closer to finding
myself.
Thank you mother, for being.

Margaret wrote this verse to express her feelings about her father's death when she was seventeen:

I see the photo of you and me
Our faces so delighted, the tree reflecting
sparkles
I seem to hide behind your waist
Poking my head around to see the wrappings
That will soon be thrown away
Your massive arm is around my small shoulder,
I'm clutching your older body for security
How were we to know you'd leave us next Christmas?

You'll never be back in this place
And I will surely give my life to be with you
But I will have to wait for the black lace to wrap
me
(As it did you) and bring me to your side

Children's outpourings reveal that the loss of a parent is a devastating experience for them. Symptoms of this experience include sadness, guilt, inactivity, and increased anxiety.

Children of Divorce

Divorce inflicts losses on a child that range from the most obvious—the loss of or the change in the relationship with the absent parent—to a variety of others that are not always so obvious. Together, however, they can add up to a major disruption in a child's life. Economic adjustment, change of residence, increased absence of the custodial parent (such as when the mother takes a job outside the home), and the loss itself of the non-custodial parent all require that the child give up some important assumptions about his or her family.

Response at Different Ages

It is difficult to assess the psychological damage children suffer as the result of divorce. The trauma can result from predivorce parental conflict, from the actual separation as well as from postdivorce adjustments.

The age of children at the time of separation from a parent is considered an important clue to how children will adjust. Preschool children typically act and talk as though nothing has changed. A toddler may continue to ask, "When is Daddy coming home?" Changes in behavior may be noted, such as regressing to bed-wetting and thumb sucking. Sensing a feeling of abandonment, very young children may externalize their anxiety by whimpering, fearful behavior. They may cling to their custodial parent—fearful he or she might leave, too.

Somewhat older children, six to eight years of age, are less likely to deny what has happened. Their reaction is sadness and withdrawal.

Eight-year-old Sarah's little face expressed more sadness and anxiety over the divorce of her parents than any child should have to feel. She was afraid her schoolmates might not want to play with her anymore. Typically, she blamed herself for her parents' separation. Tears were close to the surface and yet she found it very difficult to talk about her feelings. It was two years after her parents' divorce that she volunteered to speak of her feelings. Yet, there is still the sadness. Now, at the age of eleven, she confides, "I understand that my parents are just too different to ever live together. And it's okay because they never hassle me about my wanting to spend time with one or the other of them."

Children of nine or ten tend to be angry and may blame their parents, particularly the one they feel is most responsible for the divorce, for their distress. Lois was nine when her parents divorced and she says, "I just didn't want to believe my parents were actually breaking up. The strongest feelings I can remember are sadness, shame, and anger at them for wanting to break up our family. I was ashamed to tell my friends, and kept the divorce a secret as long as I could. I remember resenting the financial hardships we endured as a result of the divorce."

Children ten years of age and older tend to realize the impact and finality of divorce, yet they, too, suffer psychological trauma.

Nancy, eighteen, expresses her pain this way: "Mom and Dad were divorced when I was twelve. I remember feeling ashamed of my parents' divorce. I suppose I thought of Mom and Dad as perfect. The idea of divorce was new and strange to me, so I denied it and pretended it wasn't happening in my family. It took a long time before I even admitted it to my two best friends (one of whose parents were divorced, too). I just didn't want to believe that my parents were actually breaking up—it was so hard to accept. The strongest feelings I can remember are anger, sadness, and shame.

"I was mad at my parents for wanting to break up our family. I was sad because Mom and I would be moving to another state, and I didn't want to leave Dad, my older brothers and sisters, and friends behind. Being only twelve years old, I thought I was grown up, worldly, and that any change in my life would result in permanent depression from that day on."

Anne, nineteen, also suffered the pain of anger and denial over her parents' divorce. "I didn't know what was happening to my parents, but I felt something was very, very wrong," she explains. "My dad was crying, and everyone else had gone away. I went over to my friend's house, and we went out to play. We played 'kick the can' for a while. My heart wasn't in it, though; I just wanted to go home and wake up from this awful dream. My friend and I walked back to her house; it was getting dark out. We went into her house and her mom and dad asked me if I knew what was going on. Did I know? Did I want to? I know what I wanted to do—run. I wanted to shut it all out and pretend nothing was wrong, but I listened. 'Anne, your mom and dad are separating. They are getting a divorce.'

"Silence. All eyes were on me. I showed no expression as I walked out the door. I slowly went down the hill to my house and saw Dad. He was putting suitcases into the trunk of his car. I cried and shook with fear and escaped to my room."

Anne says she can't remember much about the next few days except the pain and shame she felt at school. None of her friends' parents were divorced—how could this happen to her, she wondered. She said nothing to anyone and kept so much inside. "One day a friend came up to me and said, 'About the divorce, why didn't you tell me?' " Anne recalls. "The tears swelled in my eyes, and a huge lump grew in my throat. I wasn't such an actress after all. That day was one I'll never forget, and the next day was even worse.

"Mom and I were standing in the kitchen. I was peeping through the hole I had eaten in my bologna. Mom stopped what she was doing and asked me, 'Honey, you don't hate me do you?' I answered not in words, for they wouldn't come out. I cried and cried, and we held onto one another for a long, long time. I think I missed school that afternoon. The hurt and pain this eight-year-old felt I hope I never feel again, or ever have to put someone else through. 'No, I don't hate you, Mom, but I still love Dad, too.' I said.

"When I look back, I can understand why I was so hurt by my parents' divorce. The two most important people in my life were separating. The largest influences in my young life didn't love each other anymore. I guess that's what hurt the most."

The importance of mourning in order to accept and adapt to the new conditions of life are well known. If children do not complete their mourning, they may suffer recurrent depression or a suppression of all feelings.

Children often have deep feelings of guilt which interfere with the mourning process. For example, it is quite normal for a child, when angry at parents, to verbalize such thoughts as: "I wish you were dead," or "I wish you would go away and never come back." Having expressed such thoughts can give rise to guilt when a parent leaves the family circle. Children are likely to feel it was their own hostile thoughts that caused the departure. Often children deny their loss— they do anything they can to avoid facing reality—thus, denying completion of their mourning. This is understandable when one considers children's dependency on their parents. This loss brings out feelings which may be overwhelming.

Children's adaptation to loss is complicated not only by their tendencies to distort and avoid, but also by the tendency of parents to avoid facing reality. Parents who are unable to tolerate their own loss are usually unable to help children cope. By the parents' avoidance of reality, children are taught avoidance and denial of the finality of what has happened. "Dad and Mom are getting a divorce, and Dad will not come back to live with us," are realities that children should be encouraged to accept if they are going to resolve their grief.

Children are certainly aware of conflict between parents and may feel very hostile toward the parent perceived to be the cause of a divorce. For example, Jill says, "My mother and father were divorced when I was thirteen. Much of that period is slightly foggy, probably the workings of my subconscious mind. I remember the day he moved out only as a mellow rush of relief."

Her parents' marriage had not ever been happy as far back as Jill, now seventeen, could remember. She believes her father blamed the family for his failure to obtain any of his goals in life. He had a college degree but never attempted to use it, and floated from job to job. He also was an alcoholic, like his father before him. "But he did not have to be drunk to be mean," Jill says. "He had a very strong, dominating personality and could never be pleased with any effort made by his wife or children. He made an effort—and succeeded— to seem warm and outgoing to neighbors and acquaintances, but he ruled his house as a dictator through a reign of terror. All property was actually his; things were because he said so; and if you did not do a job perfectly you were stupid, clumsy, lazy."

Even now Jill can remember her parents' arguing. Sometimes they used loud and abusive language, and on several occasions it was physical. Each blamed the other and their arguments always ended in cold silence, the only solution to their problems.

"It's hard to imagine two people living together and not speaking to each other for months at a time, but they did," Jill recalls. "In addition, I was only twelve when I first remember seeing my father hit my mother, and it was very traumatic for me. I hated him for it, and I could not understand or forgive his behavior even though the physical abuse was more the exception than the rule.

"Because of his treatment of my mother, I felt very defensive of her, and, of course, my attitude did not help my relationship with him. Furthermore, as a child I never felt that he cared for me because he never seemed to serve any other purpose except to punish us and financially support us. Once, I remember asking him why he didn't love me, and he just told me that he couldn't. Denying my hurt feelings, I responded with anger and disliked him even more, which explains why I was so elated when my parents were divorced."

Jill knew her parents' marriage was unhappy, and she felt relief when they were divorced. However, when a child has no idea that his or her parents are unhappy, news of an impending divorce can be particularly devastating. Bill, twenty-five, had believed his family was ideal. He says, "The quality of communication between my parents seemed good. Things were handled jointly, and there was real interest shown in each other's views and opinions. I really enjoyed the open-minded, happy atmosphere in which I was brought up. So the single most emotionally devastating experience I ever went through was my parents' divorce.

"The major cause, as understood by me, was that my father just stopped loving my mother after twenty-five years of marriage. The breakup seemed sudden. However, I recall on several occasions a sense of indifference with each other several months preceding the divorce. I wanted so badly to help but didn't know what to do. A few times I gave phone messages from one to the other, and I would add that the other said 'I love you' at the end of the message, hoping to patch up some of their differences. Eventually, they broke up, my father leaving with a suitcase in hand.

"I think the most painful part was that I came home as my father was leaving. I hopelessly demanded that he not leave and then my mother and I spent the next six hours in each other's arms, each consoling the other. I was the only child to actually be at home during the breakup, and I can't thank God enough for allowing me to be there for my mother's support after my father left. Those painful six hours we spent together bonded us together in a way words cannot express. For years I felt actual hate for my father. It was after these few years that I really started feeling incomplete inside. It was as if something very important in my life was missing. After much debate with myself, I concluded that my once-special relationship with my father was what was missing."

Bill said his mother eventually adjusted to the divorce, and later he and his father started to see each other again. His biggest worry was how his mother would react. "I think she realized that our relationship as father and son was important and she would in no way stand between us," he says. "Today, I have a very loving relationship with both of my parents, and I feel so fortunate to have been able to maintain these relationships. I matured immensely during this time and also got to expand my relationships with each one of my parents."

Bill feels that even though his parents' divorce was a painful experience, he was able to gain a lot of positive knowledge from it. "I learned that communication between husband and wife is critical in a marriage relationship throughout the years, with or without children present in the household. The values that I have learned from my parents and the love that I have been able to both give and get from my family have really made an impression on me regarding the importance of a loving, sharing family," he said.

Impediments to a child's adjustment are many. They almost always feel responsible for the separation and consequently feel guilty. Thus, holding on to the fantasy that what has happened is not real, or that the missing parent will return home, absolves children of guilt and helps deny the loss.

Children often refrain from asking questions or sharing their feelings about the separation for fear of upsetting the remaining parent. This inability to talk, of course, impedes the ability to grieve, for overcoming grief involves getting those feelings out in the open. It is essential that children be led to discuss their feelings of responsibility, guilt, hate, anger, and fear so they can leave feelings behind and finish their grief work.

No one talked to Liz, age seventeen, about her parents' impending divorce. "I was confused and couldn't figure out why my father wasn't living with us anymore," she said. "Hate is another word I felt during my parents' divorce. Hate and fear are one word to a ten-year-old. In my world I often saw my mother angry, I saw her swearing and throwing things at my dad.

"I coped with this situation as any insecure ten-year-old might. Many times I just pretended this wasn't happening; I developed terrible pains in the stomach and had to be hospitalized several times. I became very quiet and didn't bother anyone." Liz's grief was not explored by her parents, and some of her negative feelings eventually became part of her self-concept. "I am bad," she said to herself subconsciously, "I don't deserve anything better. My parents hate each other and sometimes I think I should hate myself just as they hate each other."

Unresolved conflict in children's minds over what happened in their parents' relationship can cause grave emotional difficulties in adult life. Liz says, "The emotional impact my folks' divorce had on me is causing me to shy away from any close relationships with the opposite sex as an adult. I'm afraid of hurting someone the way my parents hurt each other. Sure, I have gone out with many men, but I have never developed these relationships to anything more than what you could call a one-nighter. I know my younger brother feels the same way."

Because any separation involves a break in the continuity of caring that has been experienced, children's behavior will often regress, and they will externalize feelings of loss and anxiety. When children are anxious that their dependency needs may not be met, they are likely to express such feelings in concrete terms, such as concern about food, clothes, or whether they will be able to attend college. They may withdraw, have a loss of appetite, neglect school work, or change their behavior toward others.

Mike, age twenty, for example, says his life did not get on a good path for quite some time after his parents divorced. He had started being the school bully during the divorce process, and friends helped perpetuate the role. His mother had no control over him, but he was intelligent enough to keep himself out of serious trouble.

Having a tough reputation served its purpose by discouraging others from giving Mike more problems. "No one ever picked on me or told me what to do," he says. "I gradually returned to a more or less productive life style by the time I entered college. That was after dropping out of high school twice. I have been in counseling, but I believe I am making it now."

Another problem for children of divorce is that if a parent does not resolve the loss, he or she may relate to a child as he or she did to the former spouse. If a father, for example, feels bitter toward his ex-wife, he may take these feelings out on a child who reminds him of the mother. If a parent finds the solitary task of supporting and managing the children and the household frightening or distasteful, the children may be hurt or confused. As Rob, age eighteen, says, "Mom started work right away, and then she went to a business school. She had so many pressures. She never could get up to the right speed for typing and could never do her bookkeeping. When we were timing her typing, she would get so frustrated—rip out the paper and give a big scream. That led us to run outside and do something to take everything off our minds. Mom did the best she could, but between working, schoolwork, going out, and taking care of us kids, she got pretty tired. She resorted to going out because we kids were too much to handle. We were always pestering her for more attention."

Rob recalls that his mother came home yelling so often that the children came to expect it. Instead of thinking how good life used to be, they talked about how much they missed their father. "I missed the good times, and I hurt so bad," he says. "I cried, asking why my stomach actually hurt for lack of smiles and daily contact with Dad. My mom gave us all that she could, I know that now.

"I was always so angry at Daddy for leaving, even though Mom asked him to, to the point where I could cry and hit my bed at night. I know my dad loves me. He listened to me and he tried to tell me things, but I wouldn't listen. I didn't hate my dad—I really hated the way life was when he left."

Unfortunately, in a divorce, children often bear the brunt of parental conflict, being brought into disputes about custody, visitation, and child support. Mary, for example, was torn between living with her mother or father after the divorce, but that was not a new stress for her. "I lived in a family where both my mother and father cheated on each other. The time that my parents were separated was a living hell for us kids. When my mother left my dad, I had to choose whether or not to stay with him. I was very young and very confused about the whole situation. But I felt that my dad needed me more than my mother because at the time he was incapacitated from an accident.

"The greatest anguish that I suffered was when I had to make the decision of whom I wanted to live with. On the one hand, my dad couldn't take care of himself properly; on the other hand, I really would rather have lived with my mom. But she just said it was up to me. It was like I was on a see-saw going back and forth, out of control, trying to decide which side to stay on."

Because children are so vulnerable to a parent's anger, the only response open to most children is to identify with the angry parent and join in an alliance against the other parent. The loyalty conflict is so destructive that a child's whole self-concept may become confused.

Studies show a high rate of frustration among children of divorce.

One that focuses specifically on the adolescent and young adult finds that there are few pleasant outcomes from a disruption of family relationships. Common reactions of young people are keen hostility, deep sadness, and bitterness. Often such children may take out their frustrations and anger through anti-social behavior. Jill, age nineteen, says that following her parents' divorce, she started taking out her frustrations on others. "I became a raging bully and literally ruled the halls of the junior high school. I became callous and cruel to my classmates. I resented every kid who still had two parents, especially if they spoke badly of their parents. Why did my mother have to divorce my dad? I couldn't understand this, and I hated all of the changes in my life."

It is important to note that the emotionally unhealthy aspects of losing a parent are not solely related to the loss of that parent. Antisocial behavior, as well as the development of a low sense of self-esteem, can result from the tensions in a bad marriage. Discord, the lack of parental support and attention, and the inability to accept and resolve losses and changes all contribute to the deteriorating mental health of a child. One reasonable, emotionally mature, loving, caring, supportive parent can give a child a good, healthy sense of identity, although having two such parents is the ideal.

Jean is an example of a child who grew up in a supportive single-parent family. She says, "The divorce of my parents helped me open my eyes to the real world. I didn't stay hidden behind my family. I reached out for what I wanted and needed, and I feel I have matured much faster than my friends. I've also experienced having to open my life to another family when my mother remarried. I miss my dad, but when I see him every other weekend, we talk about all my problems, and that helps me feel better."

Lasting Effects of Divorce

According to a recent ten-year follow-up study of children of divorce directed by Dr. Judith Wallenstein, executive director of the Center for the Family in Transition, Corte Madera, California, negative responses such as anxiety, fear of the future, and feeling responsible for their parents' breakup, may last throughout a child's growing-up period, especially if the postdivorce family is not an improvement over the predivorce family. If the overall quality of life does not improve after the divorce, the children's adverse early responses are likely to continue because often their worst fears will be confirmed: Their parents' relationship did not recover, the absent parent does not reappear in the family circle, and the conflict between parents, in many instances, has not abated. Under these circumstances there is no reason for the child's anxieties to diminish. In fact, they may intensify.

Young adults agree that childhood and/or adolescence was in some way less pleasurable as a result of divorce, and that it forced them to take on a lot more responsibility than their peers. They feel they are survivors. They can do a lot of things for themselves and are even more independent, responsible, and sympathetic than people who have not gone through a divorce of parents. But most children and young adults wish they had had an intact happy family.

However, father absence has a significant effect on young women who are having a great deal of trouble in moving into young adulthood because they fear they will be betrayed in their relationships with men. They often despair of ever achieving a happy marriage.

Cindy's parents were divorced when she was twelve. She has lived with her mother and seldom sees her father. She says, "The impact the divorce had on me greatly affected my views on marriage. I am eighteen and find myself shying away from any close relationship with the opposite sex. I'm afraid of being hurt the way my parents hurt each other. Sure, I have gone out with many men, but never on a steady basis. I can see where my parents went wrong and I'm going to try my best to stay away from that path. If I do get married, I will work hard to keep it strong and happy. No divorce for me!"

Young men exhibit less of that type of behavior. Their difficulties lie in expressing their feelings, which is not unusual in our society. Boys, typically, are not encouraged to express their feelings in the process of growing up. "Don't cry, be brave like your daddy," they are told by adults.

Most children of divorce hold traditional views about marriage and appropriate sexual behavior. They want a monogamous, lasting relationship and do not endorse divorce. They believe people should make a decision to marry very carefully, and that before deciding to have children, the marriage should be assessed very carefully.

Speaking from painful experience, they believe divorce is much easier on adults and much harder on children.

After five years had elapsed, most of the young people in the Wallenstein study still were very critical of their parents and were hoping they would change their minds. After ten years, they tended to agree that given the differences between their parents, the divorce decision probably was inevitable and necessary. They didn't quite forgive their parents for having a bad marriage, but they agreed that divorce probably had been the only way out.

Helping Children Cope

It is clear that children need conversation with parents to help restore their negative feelings regarding the separation of their parents. But how does a parent do this?

Particularly in the early stages, children need every possible assurance that they are loved. This will make them feel more secure. Caring should be verbalized. Tell the children specific ways in which they are loved. Get them to talk about their feelings about what has happened. Convey that their feelings of anger, guilt, sorrow, or resentment are not wrong—they are normal feelings which they must try to work through.

Everyone has a deep need for a sense of emotional well-being. For children to feel good about themselves, they must certainly be assured that they did nothing to cause the divorce. Children who feel loved by their parents, even though they now live separately, and who know they are not to blame for what has happened, are better able to develop a healthy adjustment to the loss.

Most children recuperate from the effects of divorce within two years. The key to how well a child adjusts seems to be the custodial parents' readjustment. Factors that influence a child's adjustment include a parent's availability to tend to a child's emotional needs, the ability to be warm and affectionate, the amount of support the parent receives from friends and family, the financial situation, and the kinds of stress the parent is experiencing.

Studies show that the level of emotional problems evidenced by children often depends on the amount of conflict in the home. Custodial parents who are anxious and depressed increase antisocial behavior among children. Parents who lack warmth for their children, and who are unable to establish and enforce clear rules are unlikely to aid their children to adjust to the changes brought about by divorce. For example, Mike, age sixteen, says his mother has no control over him. "She yells and screams at us kids," he says, "as though we are to blame for the hard times we are having. My younger brother has turned into a little monster, beating up other children his age. When we go to our mother with a problem, she tells us she has enough problems of her own having to work in a job she doesn't like and never having enough money."

Unless Mike's mother finds a way to restore order in her life, and begins to show her children affection and emotional support, Mike and his brother will find adjustment to their parents' divorce very difficult.

Every family's problems are unique. The key, however, is that before a parent can help a child adjust, he or she must first come to terms with the loss. It is important for parents to realize the importance of communicating with their children. They must break the chain of avoidance so that their children can grow up free from unrealistic thoughts about what has happened to the family. When talking with children about divorce, the conversation must be clear and open if it is going to help them complete the grief process.

Death of a Parent

Most parents do not know what their children feel about death. They are so consumed by their own grief that they are unable to give their children the kind of help they may need to handle their feelings. Depending on factors such as age, personality, and the type of relationship the children had with the person who died, children respond in various ways to death, and the trauma they suffer will differ in intensity. If not handled well, losing a parent in childhood may result in the development of emotional and behavioral disturbances during adulthood.

Response at Different Ages

Very young children, two or three years old, are thought to have little understanding of death. They live in the present, and the idea of nonexistence is believed to be incomprehensible to them. Before the age of five, children do not perceive death as permanent—it is viewed as a departure or a sleep.

Young children take things they are told literally, so care must be taken not to speak of dying as sleeping. For example, Mary was frightened at the age of four to go to bed at night after it was explained to her that God had "taken a little playmate in her sleep." When young children are told, for example, "Don't cry. Grandpa is up in heaven where he is living in a beautiful place with no pain or hurts," they are likely to be very confused about death.

Janet had explained the death of her father in that manner to her four-year-old son. One morning Jason came out of his room after breakfast, dressed in his boots and snowsuit, and announced that he was going to go outside and run in front of a truck so he would get killed. He wanted to be with his grandfather. Janet says, "Thank God I asked him where he was going. It was then that I realized how important it was to talk realistically to my son about death. I told him that Grandpa would never come back again, and that Jason would never be able to see his family again if he got killed. Jason decided he would rather stay with us."

While very young children are thought to be unable to comprehend the meaning of death, it may be merely that they have had little experience with it. Alice was barely three when her great-grandfather died just a week after she had visited with him. Alice was told in a gentle manner that Grandpa was dead, that his body did not breathe, and that he did not need food. To clarify the difference between sleeping and death, Alice was told that her Grandpa was not sleeping, that he would never awaken to play with her. His body would be put in a box and lowered into the ground. "Won't the worms eat Grandpa?" she asked. Her family laughingly said, "No," and she dropped the subject.

However, six months later, when her grandmother was hospitalized for a short time, Alice had to be assured countless times that Grandma Jane was not going to die. "I don't want you to die because I want to play with you forever and ever, Grandma," she would say.

Sarah was three when her maternal grandmother died. She was told why she would never see her maternal grandmother again, but that Grandma could always be in her thoughts. Sarah frequently continued to talk about her maternal grandmother, but she did not seem to expect to see her, "because," she would say, "Grandma is dead." So perhaps we should not be so prone to think that very young children are unable to grasp the truth about death if they are told the truth with gentleness.

Between the ages of five and eight, children still view death as reversible. Death is sometimes seen as a wicked person or an invisible ghost that literally carries people away. Children at this age level begin to fear death and have angry feelings toward this "bogeyman" who takes people away.

Jake's eight-year-old son took his mother's death very hard and continued to look for sympathy everywhere. He had been ill as a child and had developed an unusual dependency on his mother. He seemed to use his mother's death as an excuse for his bad behavior at home and school. Yet he also seemed to have a great deal of anger over his mother's death. "Why did this have to happen to her?" he frequently cried out angrily.

Of his seven-year-old daughter, Jake says, "Our little girl seemed to accept her mother's death, although she cried a lot after she went to bed. When I went to check on the children, I would often see tears in her eyes. I held her close to me, and we talked about what was worrying her. Still, she resisted talking about her mother's death. She grew up very quickly and showed great concern for her baby brother."

After age nine, children are said to recognize that death is permanent, irreversible, and inevitable for everyone. Tom's daughter Terry was nine when her mother died. He says, "She became very quiet after her mother's death. Kept all her feelings inside. Three weeks after the funeral she began crying after she went to bed, sobbing, sometimes almost to the point of hysteria. I tried to comfort her, but finally I just let her cry and never made a big thing of it. I just stroked her head and talked a bit and then left.

"There was a lot of anger over her loss coming out. You could tell by the tone of her cry—it wasn't even a cry, it was like a wail, like the piercing cry in a horror movie. It had a message—the message was anger. She would cry until she was exhausted. Finally, I took her to a family counselor, and we had eight months of family therapy learning to get our feelings out and talk to each other."

Although older children may have more coping skills than younger children, they must still deal with new feelings of anger, guilt, abandonment, and sadness. Death-related nightmares are not uncommon. Most children at some time or other feel angry enough with their parents to wish them sick or dead, or to think of them as dead. If death does occur, the children see themselves as responsible. Twenty-year-old Ralph talks about his reactions to his father's death: "I had a pretty average childhood up until I was twelve years old. One morning my father got up for work but never left the house. He died of a heart attack. All I wanted to know was why my father died and not someone else's father. For years I found myself trying to blame someone for my father's death; I blamed just about everyone.

"First, I blamed the medical people. It took the rescue squad forty minutes to get to our house, and when they got there they couldn't do anything anyhow.

"Second, I blamed God. We all loved God and lived good respectful lives. So I said to myself, 'Why did You let him die, God? He was a good person that lived by Your rules and loved You; what kind of a God are You?' For years I refused to go to church, and I never prayed to God. I even swore at God, and I constantly had terrible thoughts about God in my mind.

"Last, I blamed myself. For years I was obsessed with the idea that it was my fault that my father died. If I got punished or my father wouldn't let me do something I wanted to do, I would get really mad at him. Sometimes I said to myself that I hated him, and sometimes I almost wished that he would die. These thoughts stayed in my mind after his death. How could I ever have thought such terrible things? I said to myself and to God that I would be the best kid ever if he would come back to life. This guilt was awful, and it took many years to overcome."

Ralph finally realized he couldn't blame others for the death of his father, who had a bad heart and a family history of heart disease. He understood the rescue squad did all they were trained to do and the hospital did all they could have. He said he probably never will be able to figure out God's role in death, but he believes and has faith in God.

Ralph, then, has gotten over the idea that he was to blame, although it took him years. "After a loved one dies, I think it is important to realize that you have your life to live and that you will have all the knowledge, feelings, and memories of your loved one to guide you through your life," he says. "You should not blame anyone for the death of a loved one, especially not yourself, because self-blame causes nothing but added guilt, pain, and suffering. Seek instead the peace of mind from knowing that none of us is perfect, and that God is all-forgiving."

Children's reactions to death vary not only according to their ages but according to whether the death was forewarned or unexpected. If a death has been expected, perhaps as a result of a terminal illness, it is generally not as difficult to deal with as one that occurs without warning. Ralph's reactions to his father's death exemplify the intense emotional and physical reactions to a sudden death.

On the other hand Edith, now eighteen, experienced the slow, painful death of her mother's dying of cancer. She says, "When I was told that my mother was ill with cancer, I didn't know what to do, or what to think. A few weeks ago, Mom was up and around, working, doing everything normal; now she was weak and full of pain. When I visited her in the hospital it was so hard to talk because I just couldn't find the right words. I was so afraid of scaring her more than she was that I didn't say anything. I wanted to tell her how much I loved her and needed her, and I wanted to tell her to fight, but I was afraid of crying in front of her.

"After some treatment, Mom came home, and I thought she was going to get better. But I was wrong. They took her back to the hospital, and she became weaker and weaker. I knew in my heart that she was going to die, but I still didn't want to face up to it.

"I think that most of my strength during my mother's illness was due to the kind of friends I had. When I cried, they comforted me. I was mostly crying for myself. It wasn't fair that I was to go on without having a mother. I was too young. I kept thinking about the future without her.

"Her condition worsened rapidly. She couldn't talk or stay awake, she was in such pain. To see my mom in such pain was so hard to handle. It was the hardest thing to stay there, yet it was the hardest thing to leave.

"I kept hoping she would die soon. And when she finally died, I was relieved, and for the first time in a long time, I could get a good night's sleep after a long cry. This is not to say I wanted her to die, because I loved her a great deal and miss her very much. I'm simply saying after the death, our lives returned to some form of normality." Edith had time to anticipate her mother's death and appeared to have no problem accepting the finality of death.

The complete shock of a sudden death of a parent tends to delay realization of the finality of death, particularly for the younger child. Jean was only six when her father died. At sixteen, she recalls the tragedy of losing her father.

"One morning I woke up at six-fifteen to loud voices and police sirens. When I came into the living room, there were all those strange people in blue uniforms and my mother, brother, and sister were crying. My mother told me that my father was in an accident and had died. I cried because everybody else was crying, but I didn't understand completely what was going on. I remember waiting sometimes for my father to come home, but he would not come because he was dead.

"Now that I have grown up, I still want to question the reality of his death—it is nice to imagine I still have a father alive. I also have noticed that I like men who are somewhat large in body structure like my father, and they are usually somewhat on the older side, which my father was when I was born."

At the age of six, Jean was unable to grasp the finality of her father's death. At that age she probably was able to recognize the fact of physical death but not its permanence. To young children, death is a departure—like the sun that sets at night, it will return with the dawn; so children look for the return of the person who died. Unable to grasp the reality of her father's death, Jean was very distressed by separation from him. Even now, at eighteen, she looks for him in other men. That after eleven years she still fantasizes about her father is an indication of unresolved grief. No one understood the deep feelings she had about her father's death. As many adults mistakenly do, the adults in her family probably assumed she was too young to comprehend what was going on.

In many families there seems to be an emotional barrier that prevents parents and children from communicating with each other about intimate and sensitive areas of their lives. Each may be afraid to open the wound for the other, so they all avoid the topic. Maybe silence gives the impression that one is getting along or doesn't want to talk. For whatever reasons, most parents know very little about how their children really feel about death or how they grieve. Nor do children comprehend the depth of their parents' grief. Some children say they are drawn closer to siblings by the tragedy of losing a parent, but communication between parents and children is lacking.

As Mary says, "We found a way to work out our grief, and now my mother had to find her own way."

Reactions

How can a parent know what is going through a child's mind? In order to help children face the reality of death and cope with grief, adults must first recognize that children, even at a very early age, will have some sort of reaction to death. They must also realize that a child's understanding of death will be quite different from that of an adult, who has more experience and knowledge about death. However, children do go through many of the same emotional reactions that adults suffer during bereavement—denial, anger, fear, guilt.

It is important also to realize that children act out their feelings in various ways. Six-year-old Jean, who was not aware of impending death, suffered from disbelief and lack of acceptance for a long time. Children are capable of experiencing grief. The grieving child may experience the same kind of emotional and physical symptoms as the adult, including insomnia, nightmares, and nausea. The child may have feelings of insecurity and fear of being alone.

Gene, a widower with several children, says that after this wife's death, his four-year-old son cried incessantly, refused to talk to anyone, and regressed to thumb sucking. His twelve-year-old son became noisy, boisterous, and abusive of other children. His fourteen-year-old son, who appeared very anxious, wasn't eating well. Gene noted few problems in the behavior of his older daughters, ages fifteen and seventeen, except that one complained of headaches because she was having trouble sleeping. All these feelings and behaviors are normal and should be understood as such. A child's love is as real as the love of the bereaved adult, and in the midst of his own grief, it is important for the widower to note his children's distress.

Parents may not expect their children to react with anger or hostility to the loss of a loved one, yet this is very often the case. For example, Scott, who was ten when his mother died, says, "At first I was angry with her for dying and leaving me. I wondered why she hadn't lived through her illness. I wondered if she died because she didn't care about us anymore. Next I blamed the doctor, and finally

I felt it was God's fault. Why did He have to take her? I was angry at myself remembering the times she asked me to do something, and I didn't. I even became angry at my two best friends because they still had a mother and I didn't."

Children have many reasons for anger and resentment. Ginny carried a deep resentment toward her father after her mother's death and went into severe depression for a year or more. She recalls, "I was eleven when my mother had to have an operation. After the surgery, the doctor told my father there were no serious problems, and we kids wanted to go right up to Mom's room to tell her how glad we were. But it was after visiting hours, and Dad told us we should wait until the next day to see her. That night Mom died unexpectedly, and I blamed my father. I couldn't feel close to him or talk to him for a long time. I know it wasn't his fault that Mom had died, or that we didn't get to see her before she died, but I was so angry that I had to find someone to blame."

Several months after her father's death, Elizabeth, age thirteen, displayed extreme hostility toward her brother, whom she dearly loved. Since David was older, his mother consulted with him about family matters, wanting to spare Elizabeth any additional worries. As a result, she began to feel left out of the family circle. One night after behaving angrily toward her brother, she cried hysterically to her mother "David has you, and I don't have anyone—I want my dad!" Once she expressed her resentment, the family was better able to cope with each other's feelings and she came to terms with the reality of her father's death.

It is important for children to express angry feelings. Boisterous behavior and noisy expressions of anger are signs that they are getting their feelings out in the open where they can be dealt with and then, finally, left behind. As Scott recalls, "After my anger was spent, I was able to accept Mother's death as something good for her. She would no longer have the pain and hurt that had troubled her for so long. My faith in God's love returned."

Dawn was angry for still another reason. Her mother died of leukemia after a long illness. "At the age of eight," she says, "it is difficult understanding why mother had to die. The thing that made me angrier was people saying that 'it's all for the best' or 'she is better off this way.' How could she be better off without me, when we were so much worse without her? What helped me was having a dad who understood my anger, and who gave me opportunities to cry and express my feelings."

June, who was seventeen when her mother died, has this to say about her feelings of guilt: "At the time my mother died I was going to school away from home. For the first few days after my mom's death, everything was rather vague. So many things to be done, people to notify, and so on. During this time I know I hadn't fully accepted death, as I thought that any time my mom would walk through the door. I cried, but for whom or why, I wasn't sure. My religious background had always told me that death was a happy moment, so why did I cry?

"I'm sure now that my fears were for myself. I was crying for my own loss, not for my mom's gain of heaven and eternal life with God. Even though religion was an important aspect of my life, I still questioned why it happened to *me*. What had *I* done wrong? For a while I experienced a feeling of guilt that I had done something wrong, and God was using my mom as punishment. I had a hard time dealing with this guilt, and I can't truly explain how I resolved it."

From a common-sense point of view, a child's anger or other emotions may seem unreasonable. But from what medical and social sciences tell us, it is important for parents to recognize that their children can and do have such feelings. It is equally important for parents to point out to a child ridden with guilt and anger that no one succeeds in being good and loving all of the time—nor does one have to be good always. A child should be told, "It is all right to get angry sometimes. What is important for you to believe is that you did the best you could, and we love you and understand how you feel." By all means, we should never let our children associate illness and death with sin and punishment. It would have been helpful to June if her family had known about her feeling that God was punishing her, so they could have helped her with her feelings of fear and guilt.

The fear of being left alone is another common reaction of a grieving child. This is understandable when we consider the panic some children inevitably experience. James, a young man of eighteen who lost his mother when he was ten, was terrified that his father, too, would die. He says, "If I heard a noise that was different or if my father was late getting home, I imagined that something had happened to him. Sometimes I would just sit in the garage where

Dad couldn't find me, and I would cry and worry about what would happen to me if Dad died, too. I began to function again, but never without thoughts about being left all alone."

How can such fears be alleviated from a child's mind? James should have been reassured frequently by his father that Dad understood his worries, that Dad's health was fine, and that if something should happen to Dad there would be many other people who would love and take care of him.

Helping Children Cope

Just as an adult needs to grasp reality and to find ways to express emotions in order to cope with grief, so children must be allowed some wholesome means for expressing feelings. They should be free to feel sorrow in their own time and manner. They should not be rushed or pushed into communicating feelings, and, most important, they should not be brushed aside in the mistaken belief that they are too young to understand or that someday they will understand. How do we know what goes on in a child's mind when, in the midst of grief over the death of someone they know, he or she is ignored?

Susan's grandfather died when she was twelve, and she still wishes her parents had talked to her then. "I was sad and felt it was unfair for my grandfather to die and my parents never said anything about it, other than telling me he died. I guess they didn't say any more about his death because they felt I understood that death is inevitable for old people," Susan speculates.

Children seem to have a way of tuning out information that they can't assimilate. But perhaps it is better to risk explaining too fully than to omit an explanation entirely. In giving an explanation, an adult must be careful to consider the needs of the particular child. Fifteen-year-old Amy, for example, says, "When my grandmother died, I was treated as though I had no feelings at all. Without any other words, my parents just came right out and said my grandma was dead and that the funeral was going to be on such-and-such a day. I thought my parents came to the point too fast. It hurt me so much. They might have made it come out a little bit easier."

Children should be told the truth, and yet we must understand that a child may not be willing to accept it. Twelve-year-old Ruth was nine when her father died. "He had cancer, and they told me that it was better for him to die instead of living in misery. I felt like they were lying, and I didn't want to believe them. I couldn't sleep nights, and I didn't care whether I ate or not. I kept confusing death with sleeping."

Unfortunately, many well-meaning people are apt to say to children, "Be brave. Show your family how strong you can be." Being told to "be brave" denies children the right to show their feelings at the time it is most vital to do so. One mother remembers her anger at friends who told her son David when his father died that he must be brave, that he must be a man now. He tried; he tried so hard not to cry that he fooled his mother into thinking she was fortunate because her son had come through his father's death so well.

Years later, David, in helping his wife cope with her anguish over her mother's serious illness, told her he would have given anything to have been able to cry for his father. At that moment, years later, he did cry.

When caught up in their own problems, it is easy for adults to miss the real feelings of their children. One man says, "You have to tell such people to lay off their clichés about boys not crying. I told my kids, 'It's rough on us losing Mother; it really hurts a lot.' I cry with my children and tell my eighteen-year-old son that it takes a man to cry." Adults cannot be reminded too often that children must be allowed to express honest emotions, whatever they are.

Many people feel one of the best ways to help children accept the reality of death is to take them to the wake or to allow them to view the body. This may or may not help. The actual impact of this experience upon a child will vary from one child to another, depending upon the age of the child, the relationship of the child with the deceased person, the emotional needs of the child, and the child's personality. Children may get some positive benefits, but they also may be harmed psychologically. For example, seeing a body lying in state may reinforce the notion that death is the same as sleep. Nine-year-old Warren says, "My family made me go to my dad's funeral, and it seemed like my dad should wake up if he loved us. He looked just like he was sleeping. I saw my father's dead body in nightmares for a long time. I hate the idea of dying."

Young people have mixed feelings about funeral practices. Most who have lost a close family member or friend say they found wakes distasteful and were angered at being forced to go through their "performance." Elizabeth recalls her own distaste about her father's funeral: "The service was very brief, and I remember telling Mother to quit crying, while my tearless brother and I sat stone-faced beside her. I wish funerals could be omitted, because seeing my father dead is not the best way to remember him. I would much rather remember the times when he came in the door with a package of smoked fish from Port Washington or how much fun we had at Christmas when we all went out, got our tree and trimmed it, and then stacked the presents under it. I would rather remember him as he was on the Saturdays when we sneaked out quietly, early in the morning, and painted pictures of the nearby lake and the ducks. Or how we went whizzing along, sailing on Lake Michigan. I wish over and over that my last view of my father had been of him like this instead of lying there in a coffin looking so unnatural."

While concluding that funeral services are comforting as a memorial, the typical response of college-age people is that wakes serve no useful purpose for them.

It is the widower's choice whether to have young children attend the wake or a funeral of their mother. He knows his children best—and he should not be afraid to break with tradition. If he thinks they will be negatively affected by viewing a dead body, or the children oppose the idea of a wake, he should support their wishes and work out an alternative way for them to say good-bye. There is no assurance that an open casket and a long, drawn-out wake will provide the positive function it is supposed to. A closed casket and a beautiful memorial service to honor the dead person may be much better. What is really needed at this time is loving conversation about the person who has died.

But how can a widowed man communicate in the way he should with his children? Many men find that although they try to discuss death with their children, it is too difficult, and in many instances they are unable to initiate conversation. Typically, a father of several teenage children says, "They just seemed to accept death. They did not grieve openly after the funeral. I have discussed their mother's death with them a few times, and they do not show any emotions. I wish I knew how to help them express their feelings."

Another father of a seven-year-old says, "Billy uses his mother's death as a sort of crutch—he seems to be looking everywhere. Yet I can't reach him." The father of a three-year-old child says, "It is very difficult to explain to a young child so dependent upon his mother what these changes are all about. Jimmy is hostile to me and seems to think I am in some way responsible for his feelings of being abandoned by his mother."

It is difficult to generalize about the best way to help our children or ourselves cope with death, for everyone's problem is unique and the thought of death appears as a threat to most people. It is not surprising that most parents put off talking about death to their children: they stall until faced with the issue. It would be better if parents did not wait until the death of someone close to talk to their children about death. When learning about sex, the trauma of the onset of puberty is much smoother if the child has been told about his or her sexuality in a loving and open manner. Similarly, the trauma of death can be softened through conversation between parent and child prior to the experience. If children see that their parents are comfortable about discussing death, they will be more at ease, too.

But, you might ask, how can I talk about death with a child if I haven't come to terms about death with myself? The answer is, of course, to reach some level of understanding and communicate with the child at that level. We must try not to give an explanation about death that we cannot accept ourselves. Few people have reconciled themselves to the fact of death. Perhaps it is not truly possible to accept its reality until one has experienced the death of a loved one. As parents, we ought to do what we can to break the chain of avoidance of the topic of death so that our children can grow up freer from their fears and fantasies about it. Unless we discuss death candidly with our children, they cannot learn that it is a reality. Clear and open communication is vital if we are to help them cope with their grief. However, communication among family members or friends is in many ways a touchy matter because it not only involves speaking, listening, and really hearing, and it also involves emotions. Communication is a sadly neglected art in many families, and given the highly emotional feelings during a crisis of illness or death, even though talking is so very important, many people are helpless in dealing with each other's needs.

Bruce, age seventeen, for example, says, "While my mother tried to shield our family from the knowledge of her great suffering, it was very apparent. I could not wish this type of agony on any living being. As I look back on my treatment of my mother with regard to hospital visits and general conversation, I wish I could have helped her by providing some kind of emotional release. I seldom talked to her about her pain. Now I think I should have been more direct. I was avoiding her in a sense because I didn't know how to react to her suffering. When she died, I know that not only was I relieved that she would not longer suffer, but I was relieved that I would not have to cope with my own inability to communicate with her."

What else can a father do to help children through the trauma of bereavement? He should assure them of his presence and love, particularly in the early periods of grief. He should try, without being pushy, to get the children to talk about their dead mother. He must give them every opportunity to review their memories. Referring to past experiences makes it easier for children to reminisce. And he shouldn't be afraid to cry with his children. For them to see that Dad hurts, too, will make them feel more free to express themselves. It is more frightening to children to be sent away than to see an adult cry.

On the other hand, children should not be urged to display unfelt sorrow. This could make them feel confused or hypocritical. It is also important *not* to convey to a child that deep sorrow is a fearful thing or something bad. Rather, it is good to point out that sorrow is mainly being sorry for ourselves because we miss the person who has died. Ron, who lost his mother at age thirteen, says, "Actually, many of our sad feelings are selfish feelings, pity for ourselves because we miss the person who died too much. They are 'I feel' rather than 'she feels' emotions. But too much self-pity does nothing but hurt everyone involved. Nothing can be accomplished by it. When we lose someone we love, the most important thing is to not sympathize too much with ourselves. We shouldn't feel resentment about a death. We can thrive on the opportunities and happiness we have had in knowing and loving this person and keep this part of her alive in our memory." In keeping with one's religion, a parent may want to assure a child that a dead person is safe in God's care.

Children have a deep need for a sense of emotional well-being. A child may find some reassurance and insight by reading a book about death. Among the many children's books dealing with death is Marjorie Rawlings's *The Yearling*, a story of a boy's devotion to a pet deer and his deep sorrow when the deer has to be shot. The boy's father cannot spare his son the pain of losing his beloved pet, but he helps him understand the reason for the pain and gives him the courage to bear it.

There are many ways to help a child cope with grief. But no matter how a widower chooses to help his children face the death of their mother, it is *very* important that they be allowed to share in the family's grief. They should not be sent away to a neighbor or a friend during preparation and mourning; this might intensify their feeling of loneliness and increase the difficulty of their adjustment. This happened to thirteen-year-old Bobby. "I really didn't know that my father was dying. No one really told me. I guessed. I wanted to catch up on all the time we had been missing since he got sick, but I was constantly told to go to someone else's house. I felt in the way and left out, and for a long time, I couldn't believe that my dad was gone."

Children need to know that life is precious and that death can come to anyone at any time. They need to be reminded that their mother can be kept alive in their own minds and memories. And they need to be told, even though they may not believe it, that their pain will diminish.

Richard, age eighteen, comments on this: "The first several weeks after my mother died, I missed her a lot. I would catch myself thinking about something that I should go home and tell her about, only to remember she was no longer there. It wears off with time, and a new pattern of life is formed to adjust for the missing member of the family. I know that I still miss her, but after a year it is not the same anymore. I have learned that death is a necessary part of life.

"My advice to anyone who loses someone he loves is to chalk it up to experience. We are created of dust, and we will return to dust. What does it matter how or when? This is the reality of death. I look at death in a much different light now than I did before. The pain is disappearing, but I don't believe it will ever disappear completely. I have lost a very important part of my life, but from that loss I have gained a much greater understanding of death and respect for life."

The following chapter examines how newly single men meet the Herculean challenge of helping their children move on to establish a new life while trying to cope with their own pain.

4

The Single-Again Man as Single Parent

HISTORICALLY, cultural values and expectations have determined parental roles. Recently, changing expectations about the role of women has created concomitant changes in the role of men, with men participating increasingly in parenting their children. Men have always cared for children under certain circumstances. Indeed, because of high maternal mortality in past centuries, widowed fathers were the original single (custodial) fathers. However, when a man had custody of his children, he was not seen as being capable of providing care for them and was often pressured into remarriage to provide a mother. Sometimes a relative became a substitute mother. In either case, men seldom identified with the role of parent.

Until very recently most American fathers have been on the periphery of the family as far as parenting roles are concerned. This is in part because of the way young women are socialized. Little Sarah receives a doll and begins to practice being a mother. She may also receive trucks, planes, cars and computer games, giving her a perception of a wide variety of roles she may fill. There has been no counterpart in terms of socialization for the male child. Toys suggest to little Tommy that he will grow up and eventually become a provider, his primary role in life.

Recent literature, however, recognizing the slight increase in custodial fathers, suggests that men, while continuing to fill the traditional family role of provider, are capably providing tender, loving care for the emotional and physical needs of their children.

Being a parent is one of the most awesome, difficult, and

responsible roles anyone plays. Because the problems encountered within each family circle are many and varied, there is no neat formula for parenting that will work for each family. We can, however, learn something from the experience of others.

In addition to developing their skills as caretakers, a big challenge for most newly single men is to help their children cope with feelings that were problematic for themselves as well, such as anger, guilt, abandonment, and sadness. Some men report major problems with discipline as their children try to cope with loss by acting out their feelings.

This chapter describes the interactions of newly single men and their children as both adjust to the reality of their new lives. We find that men are not only providers and disciplinarians, but also emotionally available parents. Although many men report finding little support or guidance for their new role as single parents, many do an admirable job, especially in explaining the divorce or death and reassuring their children that they were loved and would always be cared for. When given the opportunity, men can become parents in the fullest sense of the word. In general, fathers who share the nurturing role before the divorce or death tend to be more successful in fulfilling the physical, social, and emotional needs of their children afterward.

The Divorced Man as Single Parent

A father's options after divorce generally are: full custody, joint custody or visitation rights. We will consider first the man who has full custody of his children.

Full Custody

Divorce is traumatic for children of all ages and at all income and educational levels. Caring for children by a single-parent father can be difficult primarily because he may not have been conditioned for the parenting role. Many studies, such as one by A. Luepnitz, a social scientist, clearly demonstrate that given the opportunity, men can parent very effectively. Perhaps the greatest drawback to a father's gaining custody is the myth that men are providers and disciplinarians, not parents. Fewer than 10 percent of men receive custody of their children in the divorce courts, and these custody lawsuit decisions seem to be based on gender rather than on who is the better parent.

How and why custody is established has important bearing on how successful a man is in fulfilling the parent role. Frank is a thirty-year-old mail carrier, divorced two years ago after nine years of marriage. Here is Frank's story of how he happened to win custody of his children after a typical, almost losing battle with the courts.

Frank, the father of three young girls, says trouble began in his marriage when his wife wanted a career as a singer with a band at the expense, he believes, of her children and family. She neglected the children. She stayed out late, and Frank often found himself waiting for her to come home at 6:45 A.M. so he could leave for work. "She wanted to make a million dollars and would do anything to succeed," he says. "She got violent when she didn't get her way, and she had a drinking problem. She got abusive with me, but never with the children."

Although Frank's wife promised to quit drinking, he often found liquor hidden around the house. One time he collected three full cases of beer, although she never asked about where the liquor disappeared to. Finally Frank asked for a divorce and for custody.

"She got very angry about this," Frank says. "She accused me of getting my friends to tell lies about her and spy on her because the neighbors stood by me. I almost think deep down she wanted me to get the kids, but it's hard for me to tell."

When Frank's wife moved out of their house, she moved into an old farmhouse with no indoor plumbing, although at the pre-trial hearing she said she and her boyfriend planned to put in a toilet and bathtub. When the court commissioner said he wanted to check out her house before making a decision, Frank's wife excused herself to go to the bathroom and ran off. The court commissioner gave her a week to prove to him that she should have the kids or they could return to Frank, and at the final hearing she relinquished the children to him.

Frank said the pre-trial hearing was the first time in the custody lawsuit that things went his way. "Up until then the social workers said that while things sounded bad, they had to believe that my wife loved her children and would change her ways," he says. "It frustrated me with the whole system, seeing these so-called professionals siding with my wife and saying I had no call to take the children back into my home. Even after the whole thing was over the guardian *ad litem* said he really thought both parents were fit, and he couldn't make a judgment about custody.

"My children are now seven, nine and eleven years old—two years older than when we separated. They are very cooperative and we get along quite well. Finding baby-sitters has been my biggest problem. Some of the baby-sitters I got were married couples with kids of their own, and I would come home from work and the place would be just in shambles. On my mailman's salary, funds for child care are limited. I finally did as so many single fathers do, I had to ask my parents and sisters to look after the children while I was at work during the summer and after school during the school year. You know, the work place doesn't give a damn whether you have children to look after—you will go to work when they want you to or you won't have a job.

"On the average day, I like the mornings best. Each girl gets up separately. They wait for me to come to their room, and I make a game of carrying each one of them to the bathroom. I give them a little back rub and they give me a little hug. Then they all get dressed, we have breakfast, and I send them off to school. Then I try to get a few things straightened out before I leave for work. When I get back from work I pick the girls up and I make dinner, do the dishes, and clean up the house. I put the children to bed at 8:30 P.M. and flop down to rest for a few minutes. I might sit up and watch television or read for an hour, but by ten o'clock this parent is ready for bed."

Frank is concerned about the girls' mother's influence on them, which he feels is not good, and he knows their mother does different things to woo them—she always gives them their way and gives them treats. Once she took them to a bar at night where her band was playing and kept them out until after midnight. He thinks they naturally will pick up some bad habits when they visit her, but he tries to set a good example for them. After one visit his oldest daughter called him a 'bastard' even though she didn't know what it meant. When he reprimanded her, she said, "Well, Mom calls you that all the time."

Another of Frank's fears is the same fear that most men with custody have—that the courts might return custody of his children to their mother. His ex-wife says that as soon as their oldest child turns twelve, she is going to take the girl to live with her and her new husband, and Frank doesn't know what he will do about it. "Hopefully, my daughter will not want to live with her mother," he says, "but she will put a lot of pressure on our daughter.

"When I ask them to do something they don't like to do or discipline them, they remind me that their mother doesn't do that to them," he said. "And I don't want my twelve-year-old daughter singing in bars. I will fight to keep my ex-wife from getting custody of any of my girls, but just the fact that I will have another hassle is difficult to contemplate. In fact, the social worker saw my girls in a bar singing with my ex-wife's band during the trial, and she put this down as evidence in my favor. However, it is frustrating that you have to get so much proof to warrant having custody of your children just because you are the father."

Frank's problems and concerns as a single father with custody are typical. He provides good physical care for his children, he tends to their emotional needs for love and affection, and he had ample experience as a nurturer prior to his divorce. Yet he is reluctant to ask his children to help much around the house and worries about discipline since his ex-wife gives them none. He fears becoming the "bad guy" in the eyes of his youngsters, for there is always the threat that he may lose custody.

Frank's difficulty in finding adequate child care is also typical, as few work places make allowance for either the single father or the single mother.

Joint Custody

Joint custody is becoming recognized as a way to spare the children as well as parents some of the trauma that appears inevitable in child-custody lawsuits.

Mark, a high school teacher, is thirty-four and was divorced after ten years of marriage. He initiated the divorce after finding out his wife had a lover. "There were really tough times," he recollects. "She would go and spend weekends with her lover. She wanted me to move out so her boyfriend could come and live with her. We ended up splitting our property, and I have to pay her for her half of the house. She does not have to contribute to child support. We have joint custody with placement of the children with me."

Mark says what happened to his marriage made him terribly angry, and he was very lonely. Being with his nine-year-old daughter and six-year-old son, helped him the most, because the responsibility kept him from wallowing in his own misery.

"We are doing very well as a single-parent family. I usually had good communication with Steven, and now it is getting better with both of them. My son is beginning to talk to me more. We are getting closer just because I am doing more things for him, being the only parent on a daily basis."

Mark reports that life is easier with Steven in school all day because when he was in kindergarten, it was difficult to find baby-sitters and to get him to school. "The children get out of school at different hours, but they go over to the neighbors until I get home from work, so they are still playing with the same neighbor kids." Mark chauffeurs the children to gymnastics and has become more active in the local Parent-Teacher Organization. The family goes roller skating on Sunday nights, and on bike rides and to hockey games through his single-parent group.

"Oftentimes I get exasperated when they begin to pester about when dinner is going to be ready," Mark says. "And, then I say, 'Well, are you doing anything to help? Get in here and help a little bit.' I have to start increasing the things they do around the house. They are getting old enough. I have learned to be consistent in what I ask them to do, because if I do a chore for them one day, they expect I will do it the next day, too."

Mark and his ex-wife have had a few disagreements about the way their children should be brought up. Because she was easygoing, Mark was always the one to discipline them, although he is not always sure of himself in this area. "Sometimes when they get to fighting I get angry too fast and yell at them, and I know I shouldn't do this. Yelling doesn't solve many problems," he says. "I am trying to learn more about raising my children through reading books and attending meetings about child rearing.

"Although sometimes my daughter expresses a wish to be with her mother, I feel that I can handle that hurdle, and that my children will come to understand that being with their father who wants them is best for them. I think now that she has moved in with her lover, their mother will spend even less time with them. One time when they were over there, she had to take them outside while he was watching a football game. So home looks better and better. The kids are pretty sharp, and they know what's happening."

Mark's advice to single fathers: "It helps to get closer to your kids and really find out what they are thinking and feeling. I guess I really didn't know them before, but that is rapidly changing. Needing to spend time with the kids is important, but it is also good to save some of your time to spend with adult companions. Children do not fill the void that is there without a wife, but just the affection they show me makes me feel good about myself as a person and as a parent.

"For example, my daughter was sick, and I stayed home from work with her for a couple of days. She wrote me a note saying she appreciated my staying home and taking care of her and said, 'You're the dad that really loves us.' It really broke me up reading her loving note to me. She drew a little picture of her in bed, and me taking care of her and wrote on it, 'My Daddy loves me.' It was very touching." Mark believes his kids are responding to their love for each other in their behavior. Their grades have gone up in school, and they seem very competent and self-reliant. He puts his kids first, spending a lot of time with them. And he and his wife have protected them from a lot of strife over the divorce. There is stability in their lives, and they know both their parents love them. They have not had their loyalties torn between their mother and father. "And all this has paid off in that our children are well and emotionally healthy," he concludes.

Jack's experience with his seven-year-old daughter is more typical of a shared custody arrangement. Jack bought out his wife's half of their house, and she moved into a condo about three miles away.

Little Martha generally spent weekends and Tuesday evenings with her father. However, Jack's former wife is a nurse, and when she worked other than the day shift, Martha stayed with Jack. After three years, Jack's career necessitated a move to another state. An agreement was then reached in which Martha would spend all of her holidays and three summer months with Jack. He says, "I keep in constant contact with my daughter. We speak frequently on the telephone, and I arrange to see her every month that she is not staying with me. I don't believe we have lost any of the closeness that has existed between us since birth. Perhaps as an intern in pediatrics, I knew the importance of fathering and felt confident to care for our infant daughter. I bathed her, dressed her, took her for long walks in the evening to soothe her prior to bedtime. As she has grown older she has been as likely to turn to me for comfort as to her mother." Jack and his ex-wife believe in a certain amount of discipline for their daughter, and unlike some fathers with single custody, Jack follows an established pattern of gentle firmness without fear of repercussion. These two parents are determined to do whatever is best for the emotional well-being of their daughter. They consult each other. They remain on good terms for the sake of Martha in that they are always civil to each other. They don't use their daughter as a scapegoat or "political football" to get back at each other.

For example, Jack explains that he and his wife are determined that Martha will never be put in a position of feeling guilty over wanting to spend time with either parent. Jack says Martha tells him, "Daddy, while you lived near us, I really appreciated never having to worry about being hassled over doing something with Mom when I was supposed to be with you."

Jack says, "She wanted to stay with her mother for Christmas this year since she had been with me the past two holidays. So she will be flying in the day after Christmas in time to spend a happy week with her paternal grandmother and me.

"Maintaining a relationship with loving grandparents is important for children," continues Jack. "Joint custody not only helps to preserve a relationship between both parents, it can keep children of divorce in touch with extended families. It is important to prevent breaks in family ties whenever possible." Martha has become accustomed to living in two homes and thinks she is special having both. Jack says, "We feel an obligation to do all within our power to spare our daughter as much trauma as we can. After all, we did destroy the continuity of her family life, and this has been very difficult for her. Things are working out very well for me as a single-parent father."

What about the father who is allowed only visitation rights with his children? Let us examine his limited parental role.

Visitation

When Gerald, a university professor, asked his wife for a divorce seventeen years ago, his youngest son was ten years old, his daughter was twelve, and his oldest son was eighteen. Gerald recalls, "When

I first left and took a room in a rooming house nearby, I came by the house quite frequently to see the children. I remember the youngest, how close he stayed to me—walking like a duckling behind his mother. I was saying all the things that fathers say: 'I am not leaving you, I love you,' but, of course, his mother was saying, 'It is your father's fault that he is not living with us anymore, the son of a bitch.' "

Gerald says that didn't have much of an effect on his oldest son, but it certainly did on the younger two children. There was a period when his daughter very much took her mother's side—he was the "bastard" causing all the problems, although this has changed in the last three years since she began attending the university where he works. Gerald believes that although his daughter's siding with one parent against the other wasn't conscious, all she was hearing was her mother's side of the story. Plus, she had to live with her mother and try to get along with her.

"I can understand that, and I have been lucky that the lines of communication have stayed as healthy as they are," Gerald said.

Gerald feels guilty that he chose to work in New York for a while when his younger son was a sophomore in high school. They had been close, and Gerald felt he let his son down. "I think it hurt him that my job was more important than him, even though I probably ended up seeing him almost as much as before. I was going broke flying back and forth." The younger son will probably live with Gerald next year while he attends Gerald's university. His older son has always chosen to live with him, and his daughter is on campus.

Gerald believes the children took the divorce rather well, even though they were sad. But he feels the main problem is financial, saying he has never kept more than a third of his pay at most. He lives frugally. "My money is going to go for my kids first, whether I am ever married or not," he said. "So I don't see the divorce as a real loss, but it does mean that if I fell hopelessly in love with this year's Miss America, I wouldn't be able to afford champagne dinners and the like!"

In retrospect, Gerald knows leaving his children was the most difficult aspect of his divorce. Yet although he had limited time with them the first few years of the divorce, communication has remained good. He feels he is not intimate with his children, but they open up occasionally. "But as with most kids I know, if they have a problem, they think they have to just tough it out by themselves."

He believes with his daughter, however, that a loss has occurred and will never be made up. "She is pretty warm to me, although I think there will always be a little guardedness, for she more than the other kids thinks I ran out on them," he says. "I can't fully compensate her for it. But it's not hostility, and I think there is increasing understanding on her part." He thinks that although his children may still feel he wasn't there, that he left them with their mother, there is a growing belief that their mother was not right in her assessment of him.

"Maybe they are right—I did fail them—but I couldn't sacrifice my whole life, and the children were not being served well by living in a home full of tension and hate."

Gerald's advice to other fathers in his situation: "Keep working for a good relationship with your children, no matter how frustrating. You must keep trying to get through to them, keep doing things to let them know you love them, that you are trying to do right by them, and even if the message isn't getting through at the moment, eventually it will. Eventually the kids will get old enough, as mine have done, to see who is making it difficult and frustrating for them and their dad to get together. That won't take away all the pain, but it will soften the situation."

Gerald's relationship to his children is typical of some men who have divorced their wives. The hostility left over from the divorce causes some wives to attempt to get back at their ex-husbands through the children.

Roger, who has two sons, ages six and seven, finds that he also is unable to see his children as often or when he would like. Divorced for less than a year, he says, "At first we set up a schedule where I would see each child separately at least one evening a week overnight and see them both for one afternoon each weekend. I want to have my children with me regularly. I want to find out what's happening in their lives. I want to know how they are doing in school and to help them with their schoolwork. It has been a great frustration to find out that this could not be done this year. The court counselor agrees with their mother that I cannot have them overnight on a school night, so I have not had them overnight for quite a while. That my ex-wife has been successful in getting this ruling just galls the hell out of me."

Roger said the children's mother doesn't feed them negative views of him, but she involves them in squabbles about money more than she should. "It's so maddening to pick up your kid and have him start out with, 'Why aren't you giving Mom more money?' Then you have to explain the situation, and at their ages they shouldn't be worrying about money." Roger is also concerned that the children have free access to the refrigerator and always have treats before going to bed. His ex-wife is obese, and he fears the children are developing bad eating habits.

Roger's advice: "Don't allow your children to get involved in any arguments you have with your former spouse. Remember, in the long run, children are your greatest interest and the most important thing in your life.

"And if you can, establish a schedule for spending time with your children and stick to it. Children appreciate knowing they will see you, and when. I think the most important thing for anyone is self-image, and the child's self-image comes from both sides. If you tell a child that one or the other parent is bad, he is going to think that he is half a 'schnook.' It is very important to protect your child's self-image as much as you can."

Although both Roger and Gerald want to play a nurturing, caring role as fathers, they have both found it difficult to get satisfactory visitation rights. Yet because of their own determination to be fathers to their children, they are succeeding despite the barriers. Is the opportunity to satisfactorily fulfill the parenting role more likely for the man whose wife has divorced him? Let's examine George's experience.

Other Factors

Some other factors influencing the relationship a divorced man will have with his children are who initiated the divorce, the kind of communication he had established with his children before the divorce, and the age of the children.

George, who has been divorced two years, says, "My daughter is now twelve years old, and the divorce has not been easy on her. She was with me in the room when my ex-wife told me she had filed for divorce. She was just eight and shocked as I was. My daughter went to her room and I went with her just as I had always done since she was an infant to comfort her when she felt bad. She asked me if I wanted a divorce, and I told her that I did not. But we were both in such a state of shock that we didn't know what to say. My daughter has not expressed her feelings, and she is very quiet. I have suggested to my ex-wife that our daughter needs some therapy, but she can't see the need. I don't have any control over Cathy, but she needs help to talk out her feelings."

George says he thinks at times Cathy hopes her parents will get back together, and she is very upset about George's new relationship. He feels his ex-wife has tried to poison Cathy against him, telling her the only reason he pays child support is because the judge threatened to put him in jail if he didn't. When he is with his daughter on weekends, he has to re-establish his side of the story.

"This is a difficult time for her, with my impending remarriage, and I think she is trying to protect herself by strengthening her alliance with her mother," George says. "She will sometimes refuse to spend a weekend with me, and yet she will ask me how much time I spend with my girlfriend's children and how much I like them, and whether they like me. Then she will suggest we have dinner together, and when we do, I make certain I assure her of how much I love her." George says he is not going to force the issue, but is going to bring his daughter more into his new relationship, to let her know that he likes to spend time with them both.

When George's daughter asked what would happen to her if her mother died, George told her she would come and live with him and his new wife. Cathy then said perhaps she would just go to an orphanage. George told her, "Cathy, you just can't divorce me. I am your parent and will always look after you." He says Cathy is very open in her expressions of resentment as well as her other feelings, sometimes saying things like "How come you spend more time with your girlfriend than you do with me?" George doesn't counter with negative comments about her mother because he feels that would hurt Cathy further. "My biggest fear is that my ex-wife will succeed in breaking off my relationship with Cathy by convincing her she doesn't want to see me," he said. "I do attempt to get across the point that sometimes parents tend to distort things, but that is as far as I have gone."

George has this advice about custody: "A lot of fathers feel they have to spend a lot of money on their kids to buy their love. This is not right. I told Cathy that if I had to buy her expensive gifts to get her to love me, she could forget it. Fathers need to remember that they are parents, and they should remain in close touch with their children. Let their kids know they care for them. Kids need physical closeness. She likes it best when we sit on the sofa together watching TV, and I rub her back for her. You don't have to spend lots of money on them.

"It's particularly important that my daughter knows I love her, for she has been physically threatened by her mother a few times—so much that once Cathy called the police. However, I think that Cathy overreacted, for I don't think she has ever really been physically hurt by her mother. And I don't think I could have won custody without causing a horrible situation which would only have hurt Cathy more. All in all, I think that Cathy will come around to the realization that I love her, and will always protect her. This is the most important message a father can give his daughter."

Visitation rights do not provide an altogether satisfactory avenue to parenting, but it is clear that with effort, a divorced father can reach his children and establish a caring, long-term relationship with them. There do not seem to be any significant differences in how the wives who divorced their husbands reacted to visitation rights of fathers, compared with wives who were divorced by their husbands. One might expect the latter would feel more hostility toward their husbands and attempt to make visitation as difficult as possible, and it does appear that a contested divorce almost always leaves a residue of anger and resentment which will affect parent-child relationships. However, parents who are genuinely concerned about the emotional well-being of their children keep conflict over visitation rights to a minimum.

Phil and his wife, for example, promised each other when he first left his family that the children would never be victimized by their separation. At that time his daughters were eighteen and thirteen, and his son, eleven. He says, "Their mother had essentially raised them, because like many fathers, I was too busy as a dedicated physician to become involved in child rearing. But still I loved my children, and I think they knew that. Now I have become a weekend father, and I am no longer involved in a day-to-day relationship with them. I have had to change my whole way of thinking about how I am going to deal with my children. I have had to figure out how a weekend father can exert the kind of parental authority that will help my children grow into emotionally healthy adults."

Phil sees his young son as often as he likes during vacations because his ex-wife agrees it is good for their son to be with him as much as possible. He listens to Phil, who is able to establish guidelines for behavior at school and at home. Phil does not, however, have that much influence on his two daughters, who seldom consult him. "My older daughter, who is in college, chooses to spend a part of her vacation with me, and we are now establishing a good father-daughter relationship. My younger daughter remains somewhat aloof from me and has become particularly close to her mother. Even though she is not fed any hostile thoughts about me by her mother, she still appears to blame me for the breakup of her family. She refuses to talk with me about the divorce. I am hoping this will change. In the meantime, she has two loving parents who are determined to make the changes in our children's lives as easy to accept as possible."

When the decision to divorce is arrived at jointly, the divorced father has the most pleasant relationships with his ex-wife and children. For example, Steven, whose divorce was decided upon jointly, says his ex-wife is very good about his seeing the kids, now aged nine, eleven, thirteen, and fifteen, almost anytime. He and his ex-wife are both responsible for the children's religious upbringing, educations, and values, although he is not supposed to interfere in the daily upbringing or routine. His wife keeps them during the week and Steven has them on weekends. He feels it is a satisfactory arrangement for all concerned.

Steven believes he has maintained good relationships with his children because he has been candid with them. "The worst thing you can tell the kids is 'Don't worry about it—this is between your mother and me,'" he says. "This is one of the most traumatic things that can happen to children, and they need to be brought into the discussion. We explained everything to them—why we were separating and that I would find a nice place to live where they could always spend time with me. I told them I would always be there whenever they needed me—they could call me and I would come as quickly as possible. The kids even helped me find the place I am renting."

So far there have not been any negative effects from the divorce, according to Steven. The children's schoolwork has improved, their general health is the same, and they see him a lot. "A lot of fathers never pay attention to their kids. Well, I always did, and that has not changed. So it isn't as though they never did anything with me, and now all of a sudden I am taking them to ball games and the like," he said.

He adds, "Our kids knew for a long time that we weren't getting along, and they accept our divorce and separation are final. And, of course, they see their mother with her new boyfriend.

"I believe my ex-wife and I have created a situation that is as palatable as possible for children of a divorce. Our concern has been always about what will be best for our children. We brought them into the world, and we owe them that much. We have not allowed our children to dictate to us what we should do with the rest of our lives. We do not need their permission to date or to remarry. But it is nice when children know that their needs are being fulfilled to the best of their parents' ability."

Another factor affecting visitation is the kind of communication fathers have established with their children. Phil says he spent very little time with his children prior to his divorce, and always has had problems getting his children to talk with him. Nicholas, on the other hand, feels his closeness to his children, ages ten, fourteen, and sixteen, is because he has always communicated well with them. "My wife and I always discussed family matters with our children, and they knew they could come to us with any problem. After my wife asked me for a divorce, we agreed it was important for our children to remain in close touch with me. We sat down one evening and told them about our impending divorce and tried to explain things to them the best we could. I have been divorced for four years and have remained in close touch with my kids. They come to me openly with their concerns, plans and school problems.

"My children accepted our divorce after a short period of denial, primarily because they know they still have two parents who love them, but not each other. I believe children are more aware of marital problems than we think and, therefore, can understand the divorce decision. The relationship between my children and myself remains close, and I see no reason why it should not continue."

Nicholas and his wife have been divorced for two years. His wife has remarried, and so he has reduced the frequency of his visits. He has the children one weekend each month and during vacation periods as they desire to spend time with him. He calls them every week. "Of course," Nicholas says, "I would like to see them more often, but we must make the best of our situation, and we do."

Age is another important factor. Bob's children were one, five, and eleven years old when his wife asked him for a divorce three years ago. "I will never forget the look of horror on my eleven-year-old son's face when we told them about our divorce decision. My five-year-old daughter cried and was very sad when I moved from the house. She did not seem to understand, although now at the age of eight realizes what happened to her parents. My youngest, now four, still doesn't understand, and she doesn't really know me as a typical father.

"My wife has remarried and moved 150 miles from our original place of residence, so now I see them only about every three months, but I call them every week. When I do see them, it is fun and games, family living with lots of hugs and kisses. And I have some heavy-duty dialogue with my two older kids when they feel free to talk with me. I had an excellent relationship with the older children at the time of the divorce, and this has remained. They know I love them and will always be there to protect them. That is the most important thing I can give them.

"As the children become more aware of their mother's true character and the reasons for our divorce (she fell in love with someone else), they are turning increasingly more to me. It is important to be the best father you can possibly be, and don't shower them with material things. Your love is all it will take. And don't fight with the kids over whose fault anything was. Children seem to have a natural loyalty toward their mothers, and you may be the loser if you denigrate your wife, no matter how wronged you feel you have been."

The Widower as Single Parent

Just as divorced men become or continue to be parents in the fullest sense, so do widowers. During early stages of bereavement, widowers have difficulty dealing with the emotional problems of their children. However, most learn to help their children cope with their feelings.

A lingering death usually draws children closer to the surviving parent, and this was true in John's case. He says that at the time of their mother's death his children, then fourteen, fifteen, and seventeen, did not display much feeling, although they missed her greatly. It is John's opinion, however, that children bounce back quickly, and that seeing their mother quite ill for the last three months before her death helped prepare them.

"They didn't really tell me how they felt, maybe because their mother's death was such a natural thing. After seeing her progress toward death, they just accepted it. Maybe they were just being protective of me, but it seemed like a closed subject."

John says that although the children were closer to their mother because of the demands of his profession, he and his wife had enjoyed a good communication system with their children, and they frequently confided in him. He feels the children know their mother would want them to turn to him now that she is gone. "Although they don't talk to me about their mother's death, we discuss many personal issues such as their feelings about dating, relationships, sex, and love," he says. "Many times over I have told them how proud I am of them and how much I love them."

John, like many widowers, feels the loss of his wife has brought him closer to his children. This, of course, depends somewhat on the ages of the children and on circumstances surrounding the death.

William, whose wife committed suicide, felt deep guilt wondering if he could have prevented his wife's death. His young daughter, age sixteen, who was particularly close to her mother, made ugly accusations blaming him. His sons, age twenty-eight and thirty were supportive of William in his grief.

Stan, whose wife died unexpectedly of complications from surgery, received extreme hostility from his two adolescent daughters. When his girls wanted to see their mother, Stan requested that they wait until the next morning. When this distraught father told his daughters their mother had died during the night, he was faced with total unforgiveness. "My oldest daughter refused to discuss her mother's death for over a year," he says.

While these are unusual circumstances, most widowers whose wives die unexpectedly receive loving support from their children.

Frank, whose wife died of a heart attack, says he could not have survived the immediate shock, and later grief, had it not been for the loving support of his children.

Some men with very young children find their relationship becomes more strained. A father of a three-year-old son, for example, says, "It is very difficult to explain to a small child, so dependent upon his mother, what these changes are all about. Timmy is hostile to me and seems to think I am in some way responsible for his feeling of being abandoned by his mother." Men with children between the ages of eight and thirteen may find a relationship which is considerably closer—most problems are easier to resolve when children are beyond the age of ten. Generally, widowers find that their children come to them with problems they previously took to their mothers, just as John experienced with his children.

While many widowers are satisfied with communication within their families, some wish for improvement. Cal, a forty-eight-year-old widower with two daughters, ages thirteen and fifteen, and two sons, ages seven and seventeen, says he wishes his sons would express their feelings more, although his daughters often refer to their mother and cry openly. He says, "Communication is carried on fairly well with my daughters about their mother's death. However, it is hard still for my daughters to tell me girlish things, and it is difficult for me to understand the female logic of a thirteen- or fifteen-year-old. This is my greatest frustration. Fortunately, they have a very close relationship with their mother's sister, and I am sure they consult her about personal things they do not feel they can talk with me about. I relate to my sons quite well on a day-to-day basis even though they won't discuss their mother's death with me." This widower's dismay about communication with his daughters seems typical in that even parents in intact families find it easier to identify with same-sex children.

Fathers such as John who shared the nurturing role prior to the death of their wives are better able to help their children adjust to life in a single-parent family. For example, Dick, a forty-five-year-old father of three children, ages five to thirteen, reports, "Since they had been as likely to come to me as to their mother to give them solace, or to mend a hurt finger, what hit me most was the responsibility of caring for our children. My children and I cried together, and now that a year has gone by, we have resolved much of our sadness and are enjoying life again without their mother."

On the other hand, Donald, age fifty, says, "I have never been able to express my feelings to anyone, and I never did have a good relationship with my fifteen-year-old daughter. Her mother was her confidante. Now my daughter just goes her way, and I go mine. She refuses to do anything with me. We barely talk."

This father is unable to adjust his behavior to the needs of his daughter, for he is unable to express his own emotions and has few skills in understanding his daughter's emotional needs. It is important that a father feels he can cope with his child's emotions. Once he makes this discovery, he feels increasingly confident in himself as a parent.

Many widowers find they become more actively involved in doing things with their children. As one father says, "I must confess that I used to let my many outside activities take me away from home too often. Now I spend more time at home, and I'm really getting to know something about our children. It's great and it makes me feel great as a person!"

Most widowers say their children have become more independent, and the older children more supportive, since their mothers' death. Typically, they say, "My children have taken more responsibility for making decisions that concern themselves, seem more reliable in carrying out my wishes, and are assuming more responsibility generally for our everyday living together." One father comments, "They may be willing to help, but I found that you have to assign tasks, for they are still kids and they will let Dad do as much as he will. I have to stir them up once in a while, but generally they will do their chores with a few reminders now and then."

Most widowers find their children help more around the house. Typically, they report, "Our older children are contributing more to the physical maintenance. They try to clean their own bedrooms and the bathroom, they vacuum and dust, and they are trying to learn to cook and shop." The father of a seventeen-year-old daughter says, "She is really something special. From a little scatterbrain, she is now assuming much of the responsibility of keeping the household together."

Just as the problem of receiving additional help around the house proves to be minor, so does discipline. The father and the children have suffered a similar loss and share similar pain. Thus, children seem to sense the importance of cooperation. However, whether discipline becomes a problem depends upon many factors, such as the attitude of the parent, as well as his previous approach toward discipline.

For example, Gary remarks, "I was brought up in a family that was not very strong on discipline, so in our family my wife had to be the disciplinarian. After she died, I found discipline a very difficult problem. My wife was a perfectionist, so the house always looked very nice. After she died, I rode the kids all the time to do this or that—to pick things up, to straighten things out. They responded by saying, 'Gee, Dad, you are so grouchy all the time. What's the problem?'

"Then it finally dawned on me, hey, wait a minute—I am at work all day, the kids are in school all day, and before, my wife used to be home all day and she had time to keep everything neat. So how could we keep the house up the way she did? The fact was that we couldn't, and when I realized this, I began to back off from my demands on the kids and my unreasonable discipline practices. Now the house is certainly kept less than perfect. Kids are kids, and if I ask them whose turn it is to do the dishes, they may need a little reminder, but that is all. I have learned to be very specific about what I want from them."

Many widowed fathers report few, if any, significant changes in the school performances of their children, except for the better. For the most part, teachers are aware of the state of bereavement and are supportive of the children as they adjust to the changes taking place in their homes.

However, Gary found that his wife's death had a negative effect on his children's school performance. "Their mother's death and subsequent grieving," he says, "affected all my children in school. My oldest just got through on a shoestring that year his mother died. The second one got passing marks that year, but nothing to brag about, and our youngest child was a disaster. His grades just went downhill. He still does not seem motivated to bring up his grades. I grounded him for a whole semester—he had to do his homework first before he could go out to play after school. That time his grades improved, but the minute I back off on the pressure, his grades will slide downward. That first year, he would say, 'Dad, without

Mother I just don't feel like studying.' I accepted his grief as a reason for poor grades for that first year, but now I feel he must get down to business with his school work. I told him when he gets passing grades, then he can play soccer."

Many fathers say they become more involved in such school activities as attending Parent Teacher Organization meetings and consulting with teachers. Jim says, "I had never gone to a school meeting before, and I felt as strange as hell the first few times. But now I enjoy going. I find that I am very welcome at school functions, and my kids think it's great."

Actually, most widowers express great satisfaction with how well they and their children become socialized into their new life-styles. They enjoy looking after the well-being of their children and are proud of their children's behavior. John offers this advice as the best way to make the transition from a two-parent family to a single-parent family:

"You have to go on pretty much as though it was the way it was before—the children have to go to school, the house has to be kept up, you have your work—and it all seems insurmountable for a few months. That's normal. I told myself that I would give myself at least a year to just keep things running tolerably well. I am reaching the end of that year, and feel that I have done fairly well. I have done no new projects around the house, just tried to get the day-to-day things done and didn't worry about anything else. It is not wise to make any big changes in your life-style. Don't sell the house. Get yourself a good cleaning lady to come in once a week to change the beds, clean the stove and the floors and the like. Don't mind if the house is a bit messy. The children are expected to keep their rooms orderly and to keep some order in the house or their allowance is reduced. And I absolutely draw the line on any physical activities that would harm the house or others. I learned to cook and to organize chores, and I expect the kids to help as much as possible."

As in dealing with their children's emotions and behavior, providing child care does not pose an insurmountable problem with those fathers who had previously been involved in it. Single fathers usually find they must cut back on activities as a simple adjustment to the reality of life for them. But this is not to say every widower is satisfied or happy with the necessary adjustments. For example, Ralph says, "I had to cut down on the volume of my professional and community activities upon becoming a single head of a household. I found that I began to regret the need to realign my resources. I must admit that at times I find myself resenting the pressures of being a single parent." This type of resentment now and then happens to most parents.

Bob, a young father with three children ages eight, nine, and eleven, was panic-stricken when his wife suddenly died. He says, "I didn't know how I was going to function—not for myself, because I am a survivor, I have gone through many tough situations—but how in the world was I going to raise three children by myself? Fear and panic were present, but these feelings were tempered by my children's needs and by my realization that I had to keep the family together. I think I would have done lots of crazy things if it had not been for the kids. They helped me gain a proper perspective about what had to be done.

"Actually, when my immediate grief subsided, caring for the children was not that difficult because I had always been involved in feeding and bathing them, helping them with their school work and seeing to their discipline. So I was more fortunate than some men who had never done any of the child caring before. The difficult thing was planning and getting things done. I could not reduce my work hours, but I did reduce time spent with various hobbies to have more time for my children. I must admit there were times I resented having full responsibility for my kids."

Age is another important factor in the issue of child care. Widowers with older children report a minimum of problems. Generally, when there is an age spread, child-care chores are temporarily distributed among the older children until other arrangements, such as finding a full-time housekeeper or baby-sitter, can be made. School-age children are cared for after school by friends or relatives until the father comes home from work.

In many cases, widowers left with very young children and minimal economic resources face a crisis. One thirty-year-old father says, "When my wife died, my children were fourteen months, and three and five years old. The problem of finding baby-sitters to watch the children and someone to care for the house was a nightmare. This has been a do-it-yourself project since my wife's death, but I am managing now with the help of my parents. Maybe everyone is right—telling me I should hurry and remarry." Widowers with very young children cope with child care in a variety of ways: with assistance from grandparents, other relatives, and friends; through their own previous child care experiences; and through their ingenuity and willingness to be an effective single parent.

Success in parenting enhances these widowed fathers' sense of competence and aids in reducing their loneliness. Typically, these widowers say, "If you have children, do everything in your power to let them know you love them. Cherish them, give them your best shot at caring for them. Your children in turn will give you strength, and you will increase your sense of effectiveness as a person. I needed my children to help me overcome that black feeling of aloneness after my wife died. Loneliness is the worst pain of being a widower, but I wasn't really alone. My children were with me. They were there helping to occupy my time. Of course, the children could not resolve my longing for a woman to share my adult feelings, but they certainly helped! Taking on the responsibility for my children's care has given me a sense of growth as a person. I feel good about myself."

There is little question that widowers can fill the parenting role very effectively. While men may find it difficult at first to recognize that they can be tender, loving, caring people with full responsibility for their children, they generally succeed in accepting this change in their identity. Custodial fathers are unable to escape the demands of their work because they are the sole support of their children, and the business world in general is not sympathetic to a man's role as parent, relative to the consideration a working mother often receives. When a mother calls to report an illness of her child, for example, it is usually expected that she will stay home and tend to her child. A man, on the other hand, is expected to arrange for a female substitute to care for his child during times of emergency. In fact, he himself may expect that he cannot remain at home, so indoctrinated are men to the role of "worker."

As Gary says, "Caring for children as a single parent is a big task. When my wife died, I was left with three sons, ages fifteen, eleven, and nine. You work out a schedule and keep with it. But when a child becomes ill, or is in some crisis situation, being a parent becomes a crisis itself in trying to find someone to care for your child while you must be in your work place. Usually I am able to leave for work after my children have left for school, and they stay with a neighbor after school for two hours until I get home from work. Now that my mother lives in the vicinity, this problem of child care has been resolved.

"I did the best I could in scheduling time for my children along with the demands of my work place. I used to be very hard on myself, feeling guilty if I took any time just for my own pleasure away from my children. Now I say to myself that I am doing the best I can under the circumstances. You have to be very careful not to be too hard on yourself. We never give ourselves enough credit. I tell my children that none of us is perfect, that I try to do my best, and if I make a mistake we will work from that point.

"I had to get hold quickly because of my children and my job. I felt a great responsibility for my children and for my job, which I have had for sixteen years. Now everything is on my shoulders. Whatever I do, wrong or right, is still my responsibility. So I had to get my own emotions in control, and I did seek professional help. I am glad I did. I love my three children, and I work all day at a job I enjoy. Yet when I come home, I am on a child's level. And even though I work with adults, I needed conversation and consultation with a professional counselor, someone I could talk to about my children, my work, my feelings, my hopes for the future. I believe it is imperative to get professional help when you find you are unable to cope with your grief and the stress of adding the responsibilities once handled by your wife to your own repertoire or roles."

Gary's final message is to listen to the children in order to understand their needs and to do things with them. He feels it is also important to start dating again when the grief subsides. But he cautions about being careful not to lose the relationship with the children. "It is so easy to lose contact with your children because it is often hard to understand them, especially teenagers," he says. "But if you can keep a line of communication open—which is extremely important—then I think you can conquer most anything regarding your relationships with your children. You must be firm with them. I reminded my kids that we were four, not five anymore, and that to be a successful team we must always do our own chores and to cooperate with each other. I know there are times when it is easier to do it yourself, but then you are not teaching them anything."

Problems vary from family to family, and when problems become overwhelming, it is important to ask others for help and to remember that parents and other relatives offer only stop-gap solutions. Certainly a hurried marriage in an attempt to solve the problems of child care and housekeeping is not the answer. It is better to turn to the various social services that are available in most communities.

A call to a United Community Services Agency can give you a listing of various specialized services in your area, such as:

Preschool Nurseries. These provide various types of child care for the very young child.

Child and Family Centers. These offer parent education, preschool education, and day-care services; nutrition programs, transportation to and from the centers; medical, dental, and psychological services.

Public Health Services. These offer help with many types of health problems, such as proper diet and health care for the children as well as for adults. Single fathers often need information about proper nutrition and meal planning and may need to become aware of the importance of routine medical and dental care.

Children are likely to have increased illness during bereavement, and may exhibit separation anxiety as a response to loss. They may lose their appetite, develop insomnia, and show signs of depression, nervousness, and fatigue. When such symptoms occur, a parent can receive advice from a public health nurse, who, in many cases, will come into the home.

Single-Parent Organizations. Solo Parents and Parents Without Partners are organizations that may be sponsored by and contacted through churches and the YMCA/YWCA. Some groups are listed in the telephone book, and meeting dates are included in local newspapers.

Probably the most difficult question facing widowers is how to preserve their own individuality and independence, as well as be the best possible father to their children. "How do I remain independent without my children thinking I ought to do things differently?" asks one widower. Another asks, "Would my children resent my association with a woman?" One man says his younger children seemed to resent most activities that took him away from home, while his teenage children worried about his getting married again.

On the other hand, others find that their older children are happy to see them engaging in outside activities and beginning to date. The son of a widower says, "I kind of got a kick out of my dad. He acted like a young kid about eighteen years old. First he went to a couple of meetings of Parents Without Partners. You know, he had to be a good father now. And then he started going with a lady who used to be a good friend of my mother's. It was fun seeing him act like a lovesick puppy. When I think back after my mom died, I remember wondering when this old duffer was going to meet someone new. Dad was forty-two when Mom died, and I surely didn't want him to live alone."

Some widowers say their children try to prevent any new attachments at first, sometimes out of loyalty to or love of their dead mother, some out of possessiveness of Dad, or some in plain resistance to change. And it is possible that a child may genuinely believe that remarriage at a particular time with a particular person will or will not be good for the parent. Perhaps it might be good to remind our children that we don't have to ask their permission to date again or to remarry.

"Bring the children into your plans, but don't let them dictate. Be fair, but firm. They must participate in the everyday operation of the home. They must know that you value their views. They must know that you do have a life of your own to live, in addition to your role as father," concludes one widower.

While it is important for the newly single man to meet his children's physical and emotional needs, there comes a time when he must care for his own needs for love and companionship with an adult woman. The next chapter considers those needs.

5

The Return to Normalcy: Socializing and Dating

For most formerly married men, getting back to normalcy means re-establishing social ties with friends and, ultimately, dating. Contrary to common belief that newly single men have few, if any, problems re-establishing a social life when they are ready, in fact, a surprising number are considerably more isolated than they were as married persons. Because many are accustomed to having their wives act as social secretaries, they are at a loss as to how to establish their own social relationships. And beginning to date again raises its own set of complex issues.

Divorced Men

Most formerly married people at some time or another feel the need for a relationship with a member of the opposite sex. Many newly single men find sooner or later they experience the fifth-wheel syndrome—omitted from the invitation lists of their married friends. This is further complicated by former friends who often feel they must "take sides" to maintain a friendship, to choose one ex-spouse over the other. In many cases friends remain more sympathetic to the wife, regardless of what prompted the divorce, perhaps because women are supposed to need more sympathy and help.

Daniel says, "What few friends we had either dropped both of us completely or turned their sympathy toward my ex-wife. At first, I felt like I was Alice in Wonderland jumping into the rabbit hole and that I was entering a new culture—this divorce culture. I felt like a participant observer where the values are quite different—certainly quite different from what they were when I was married or single prior to marriage. I decided I needed to be with other people so I could make new friends, so I joined a group of singles and began to find this new culture quite interesting. I think if you can approach being single again from a positive point of view—hey, okay, if you are handed a lemon make lemonade, I didn't choose this, but let's see where I am—you will get along all right.

"I went through periods where I felt seventeen or eighteen years old again. I went through a whole series of casual relationships. I was like a revolving door—in a relationship for a couple of months and then out. Then I went through the grief process again—feeling depressed, angry, shocked, denying what I was feeling. I began to think I was almost enjoying being in the state of shock. Then I knew it was time to seriously think of getting back into the paired world. The advantage of joining a singles group is that it makes it easy to meet women to date. I still felt scared when I accepted that first invitation from a woman who sat next to me at a social event. It is just frightening entering the dating game after so many years of marriage. You forget how to ask a woman for some adult companionship, but at first that is all you are thinking about—companionship."

Thirty-eight-year-old Jim, divorced for two years, recollects how he felt after his wife left him, "We never made many close friends as a couple because we moved around so much. After the divorce, our friends divided their loyalty, and she still keeps in close touch with them, but I might get in touch once a year through a Christmas card. I knew I had to become involved with other people, but this was difficult because I had moved into a dormitory on my campus. But I didn't want to be alone—not just because I wanted companionship, but because I have always loved being around women. I much prefer their company to men's. For six to eight months I went out with groups until I began to date a woman with whom I developed a good friendship—I wasn't looking for anything else. Sex is not the only reason for finding female company—it is a valid reason, but early in the divorce process, friendship is more important—feeling you are back in that coupled world where you want to be."

Many men who are divorced by their wives feel a strong need for group support to overcome their feelings of rejection and to regain their sense of masculinity and a readiness for female companionship. For example, Jason, a forty-five-year-old physician, says his sense of self-worth was at its lowest after his wife left him. He explains his return to normalcy in the following manner: "I reached the point where I doubted if I would ever want to risk falling in love again. I doubted even more whether any woman could find me attractive. I tried the bar scene, but finding a pick-up to sleep with only seemed to lower my self-esteem. After this 'crazy' period, I lost all interest in sex or in dating. There was a six-month period of feeling sorry for myself before a friend insisted that I attend a support group for divorced persons. Meeting other men and women in the same boat helped me gain a healthier sense of self. A year has gone by since that first group support meeting. Several women have shown an interest in me, and I have my eye on a very attractive lady about my age. It's been twenty years since I asked a woman for a date, but tonight I'm going to grab that phone, dial her number, and hope the answer is 'yes.' "

Henry's wife divorced him ten years ago. He is fifty-six and has no desire to remarry. However, his sense of masculinity has been restored and he is enjoying female companionship. "That's all I want," he says, "women friends to accompany me to a movie or dinner now and then. I masturbate for sexual release. My work requires considerable travel, and I enjoy my freedom to come and go as I please now that my children are grown. I feel okay about myself thanks to a support group for divorced persons sponsored by our church. I had tried to commit suicide as a way to get back at her. My pastor counseled me then, but prior to my attempt to take my life, no one seemed to realize the extent of my emotional pain—how desperately depressed I was. I needed the support from our church group to survive, particularly during the early stages of separation."

In contrast, most men who initiate divorce do not feel such a strong need for group support. They often seek individual therapy to deal with their anger and guilt, but their sense of masculinity appears to remain intact. Ralph, for example, a forty-year-old university professor divorced five years, says, "At first you sort of drift around, and you find yourself doing things with new people. What was difficult for me was just finding people to meet. Most of my colleagues were married, and the married friends I had prior to the divorce no longer included me in their social groups. If finding female companionship is uppermost in your priorities, then you should get into a location or situation where there are women who would share your interests and whose interests you might share.

Ralph feels that groups are not for him. He went to a few and found too many women too eager for a relationship that he did not want. "Finding something where you have common interests has to be something almost natural and spontaneous—if you go out looking for happiness, it's like the high school kid who goes out cruising on Saturday night because he wants to get laid. The harder he tries, the less luck he's going to have. I found the singles groups to be uninteresting, doing fairly uninteresting things." Ralph also suggests it's not good to get sexually involved too soon, saying he was such an emotional mess, he wouldn't have been a good risk for a relationship.

"There were many times I wished for a woman companion with whom I could be close enough to strike up a friendship, not for thoughts of remarriage, or for sex, but just to have a relationship in which I could feel comfortable and warm," he says. "I don't particularly relish 'single life in a double bed.' A man is not always looking for sex—he sometimes wants just to be able to reach out and touch someone, a sense of intimacy, friendship, companionship—whether women believe this or not!"

It is apparent, then, that sooner or later most single-again men desire the company of women and want to re-enter the coupled world. Some accomplish this through becoming involved in groups, others through becoming involved in organizations or activities which they enjoy, hoping to meet a woman there with similar interests. There are many ways to regain a social life. What is required is taking the initiative to meet other people who will fill one's needs for friendship and companionship. This can then lead to fulfilling the need for love and sex.

Widowers

Widowers also must prepare to re-enter the paired world and fulfill their normal desire for a relationship. And just as divorced men experience reduced contact with the friends they had as a married couple, so do widowers. Richard, for example, a middle-aged carpenter, says, "What amazed me most after my wife died was the way people stayed away or refrained from contacting me after the funeral. It was almost as if I lived in a strange town. I guess people don't know how to act or what to say. My wife and I were both active in social affairs. We had lots of friends, but everything was done as couples. I get feedback from friends asking other people about me and wondering how I am getting along. But very few, even several months after my wife died, make it a point to visit, contact, or call me. I know they like me and are concerned. I know they loved my wife. We were known as the ideal couple, and were included in more things than we actually wanted to be.

"I don't think our former friends are aware that they are avoiding contact with me, but I think I remind them of the inevitability of death. Given the taboo on the subject of death that exists in our society, it really is not surprising that people want to avoid me. It is almost as though by ignoring death, it won't happen to them."

The widower is often at a loss to understand his friends' hesitancy and awkwardness toward him. Daniel, a recently widowed man of twenty-eight, comments, "The only answer is death education to prepare people for their own death and to help them understand what it will mean when someone they love dies. Why should I have to add to my grief the burden of my friends' inability to deal with death? But I do. I try to act natural, you know, brave, as if nothing has happened. If only my friends could openly express their sorrow to me and let me express my feelings to them. It would help, too, if they could think of me as a normal person with the same need for companionship with them as before my wife died—even, perhaps, more so. I am thankful that many of my friends do."

The awkwardness people feel toward the widowed is not one-sided. Daniel is finding it very difficult to go alone to social events, even in his neighborhood among old friends. "My loss becomes so apparent to me when I am with married friends—how can it help but remind my friends of my loss? It's no use to pretend I am not a reminder—rather let's believe that life goes on and it must," he says.

Other reasons exist for the isolation of the widowed. Adult society thinks in terms of couples. Hostesses believe that the symmetry of their table settings would be askew if dinner guests number five instead of six! And many widowers find that husbands are threatened by having an extra man around. A solution, of course, would be to have an extra woman, but for some reason it seems simpler to invite only married couples to a party given by married folk.

Ours is also a family-oriented society, and a whole family means one with a mother and a father. It is sad that single-again individuals must suffer the "fifth-wheel syndrome." But equally unfortunate is that whole families tend to ignore families with only one parent. Bruce, a father of three young children, angrily says, "I feel that my children are missing a very normal part of their life, namely, meeting other people in social situations. I want us to be invited to homes where a mother is present, but this is not happening. In fact, I have noticed that the friends my thirteen-year-old son is making in his first year of high school are largely from single-parent homes. The isolation from the married-couple circuit is very real indeed."

Not only is this a paired society, but no clear-cut traditions or customs have been developed on how to behave toward the formerly married. A widower is perceived differently by different people. Many look at him as the debonair man about town, self-sufficient and possibly a threat to other men. Married women may see him as someone eager to make a pass at them. Mark, for example, tells one of his experiences as a bachelor father: "I remember one day I was hanging sheets on the line, and I began chitchatting with a neighbor lady. After a few minutes, I invited her over for a cup of coffee. She looked at me as though I had struck her, and she turned and practically ran into her house. Really, my only intention was to have a conversation with her. This is something that bothers widowers— living in a community where women don't know how to react to a formerly married man. I could talk to the men working in their yards on weekends, but most women just don't know how to take a widower."

Others see widowers as sex-hungry. Ben, in his seventies, recalls a remark that came his way: "What do you do now to take care of yourself—or do you get so every woman looks good to you?" He goes on to say, "And some women, too, get pretty aggressive. These women aren't ashamed to let you know they would like to spend time with you in your bedroom. Maybe some men pursue this stuff, I don't know. I did not go for it. Sex without love isn't much."

Although many widowers despair over their social isolation from married friends, not all have that problem. Ben found that good friends remained close after his wife died and he remarried. He says, "They have always done what they could for me, those friends of ours. Of course, at my age, many of them are dead, but I never felt left out by my married friends. This didn't stop me from feeling all alone, though."

Other men claim they have been pursued constantly, particularly by divorced and widowed women. Mark says that just two weeks after his wife died, an acquaintance began bringing desserts for his family's dinner. She made a pest of herself, and he finally told her he couldn't accept her kindnesses any longer. He comments, "And then there was the young gal who began inviting the whole family over for dinner. She was interested in me, but I was not interested in her— it was just two months after my wife's death. If women think they are the only ones who get propositions, they are very wrong!"

The widower has great adjustments to make in his life when his wife dies. Regardless of how friends and family react to him as a single man, he must find his own way into a new life. As Daniel says, "I do believe that keeping busy soon after the death of my wife helped take the edge off my grief. I think old friends have their circle, and the sooner one develops a new set of friends the better. If not, one will feel everyone is against him when old friends prefer to associate with married friends and start leaving him out of their plans."

Some men turn to organized groups to provide them with a social life and an opportunity to meet new friends. William, a thirty-five-year-old high school teacher, said, "I drove myself into getting out and seeing people and joining groups. I remember the first time I went to a single-parent group, I found myself fighting back tears. And after the program was over, we all went downstairs to the recreation room and bar. There were about two hundred people there having a good time, and I thought, 'This thing lacks dignity.' Then I told myself, 'Shit, I'm the one who is out of step, life does go on.' I had to push myself into doing it, but I did sign up for several activities that evening. I realized that the alternative to getting involved with others was loneliness, and I had had enough of that. But I am still goddamn resentful about our married friends. Since my wife's death the invitations have stopped, and now most of my friends are new ones. I have met them through the various groups I have joined. I also used various dating services which are listed in the yellow pages of the phone book."

Some men, however, do not care to join social groups. Samuel, a sixty-eight-year-old professor, says, "We had good friends, and they still try to stay close, but I see them very infrequently now. I get the feeling, and I may be wrong, that they don't quite know what to do with me—how to handle me. Now when they do invite me, it seems to bother them when I come alone—though it doesn't bother me.

"I have been dragged to a couple of singles groups, but I resented what went on—complaining, dredging up the past, hanging on each other's shoulders, blaming—and I realized I didn't want to continue to roll in my grief. I'm a reasonably intelligent person, and I faced my situation and made the best of it. Let's not be morbid. Some people may need a group, but I didn't. There are many things in life I enjoy: giving small dinner parties, going to a concert, seeing a good play, or riding in the country to enjoy the beauty of nature. I can be as busy or as lazy as I care to be. I enjoy single life. My children have been my greatest support, but I don't lean on them for my social life."

Some men find new friends through work. Several younger widowers say the single women in their offices seemed quite willing to offer them companionship. Others turn to matchmaking friends and relatives. Peter, a handsome, forty-five-year-old widower, says, "Within a year after my wife's death, my sister began inviting me to dinner to meet various women she thought I would like. I finally told her, though, that I would prefer to do my own looking." There are many ways to develop a new social life. But however a widower gets back into the business of living, the important thing is to get started.

6

A Man's Need for Love and Sex

D IVORCED men appear to move into sexual activity more quickly than widowers. Widowers may feel more guilty or disloyal to their wives when they desire an intimate relationship than divorced men. They feel free to enjoy the company of women, and society expects them to, particularly if they are younger than fifty.

Several problems, however, plague newly single men regardless of circumstances. The myth about the "dirty old man" (which is untrue and unfortunate), follows both widowed and divorced older men. Also, some men are unable to perform sexually, although this usually is not due to physical impairment. Rather, impotence is a matter of mind.

The need for sex varies among men depending on their previous marital sex life. Widowers who enjoyed good sex in the context of a loving marital relationship indicate a greater degree of guilt when they first desired sex than do men who had an unsatisfactory sex life while married. With few exceptions, most divorced men feel their sexual relationships with their wives were poor or nonexistent, although that is not always the primary cause of a divorce. It may be for this reason that divorced men become interested in sex shortly following separation—they are free to find a good sex partner.

Men's emotions have a great deal of control over their ability to function sexually. In other words, the mind is the significant sex organ. As some men say, "If you don't use it, you lose it." Most divorced men report few instances of anything but temporary impotence, whereas impotence may become a real threat to some widowers after many months of sexual inactivity. Several widowers and divorced men recommend masturbating for sexual release.

Depression is another significant cause of lack of interest in sex, according to some men. Those whose wives divorce them suffer depression equal to widowers, and their desire for an intimate relationship does not usually appear until they complete the grief process; that is, work through their anger, denial, feelings of rejection, and sadness—just as is necessary for the widower.

Widowers find casual relationships largely unsuccessful in making them feel attractive and desirable as men. So do separated and divorced men.

Divorced Men

As a rule, divorced men begin to date sooner after the loss of their marital relationship than do widowers. Men who divorce their wives meet women through introduction from friends or on their own. On average it takes them three months or less to begin dating. They feel freedom, and few feel any guilt about dating. Men whose wives divorce them, however often are so filled with psychological pain that completing their grief process takes longer and delays their desire for female companionship. Many feel so emasculated after being rejected that they doubt their ability to find a woman who would want to date them. Most of these men meet their first dates through group meetings, which make it easier. It takes from three months to two years for them to begin dating.

For example, Peter, a physician, forty-five years old and divorced for six years, says, "It took me about six months after my wife asked me for a divorce to begin to date a woman I had known before from work. She was younger than I, and after a brief affair, we just drifted apart. Then it was more than six months after the divorce was final that I began going out at all, and then it wasn't all that much. It was difficult to get started dating after twenty years of marriage.

"My wife and I didn't have many problems over sex. That was about the one thing we didn't fight over. So I came into my post-marriage career without having had a whole lot of bad experiences with sex. The bad memories had to do with the fact that my wife left me for another man, and I had a reluctance to be put in a position of being rejected again. When I did start dating other women, I guess sex wasn't something I was either driven by or anxious about. And that has been the case in the last several years."

Peter has advice for any formerly married man: "Don't worry about sex, which is like telling someone with a toothache not to worry about it. But you can overcome both needs. I think sex is like riding a bicycle—you're not going to forget how, and you are going to go through periods when you probably are depressed for other reasons—worried and anxious about other areas in your life.

"Don't think that because you're not sleeping with someone or that you haven't for some period of time that it's necessarily going to be difficult when you want to start up again. There were times when I was so hung up over worries about my kids that, literally, a young state beauty queen lived in the apartment above and I didn't care who lived up there. I had my own problems. I didn't have the slightest interest in sex. Now I think, boy, I certainly missed an opportunity there. Things will come back. Just relax about it for a while and don't be uptight."

Peter also suggested not trying to have it all the first year after a separation. He says formerly married men should take their time, decide where they want to live, whom they want for friends. "I tried the singles-bars route, picking up gals for one-night stands," he recalls. "It didn't fill my need—it soon became very distasteful, and there is always VD to think about.

"I am reasonably comfortable in my single state, but that doesn't mean that I don't feel there are some things missing. Still, I don't regard them as essentials. Sure, it's nice to be able to love, nice to have a loving relationship, but there are several ways you can have love. You can love friends, and you can love your children, which I do. There are times I could feel some loneliness, but to be honest, maybe I have forgotten how good an exclusive, loving relationship could be."

George joined various single groups when he first began to date. He says, "The truth of the matter was that I bought a book about the divorce experience and took the advice that it gave to divorced persons. That was about nine months after my divorce. I really was looking for someone to talk to about my divorce when I first began to date. But after a while you get kind of sick talking about one another's divorces. And then you go on to other things, like sex.

"What I wanted out of dating was to be appreciated, accepted as

I am, where I could just be myself. I basically want an emotionally warm relationship. Within three or four months after my divorce my desire for sex arose. I didn't have any problems with sex, although I worried since I had not had much sex for years with my wife. As it turned out, the first woman I dated liked all the things I did to her that my wife always abhorred and would never let me do. In fact, she liked my sexual performance so much, the first gal I had sex with wanted to marry me right off.

"From my experience, it is very easy to have a sexual encounter. Go to a singles group to meet women, and usually on the second or third date they will proposition you for sex. Even one-night stands are acceptable to women. Lots of educated women go for this. So all you have to do is attend a singles-group party, and you will find someone to have sex with. It is unacceptable to me to have a one-night stand, but it is available if that's what you want." George said he took about nine months to begin dating.

Roger, who initiated his divorce, took far less time. He says, "I probably did more dating than I should have. I did too much socializing, at least in the beginning of our separation. As soon as we were separated I began dating. I waited a week to make sure my feet were on the ground. But I really wasn't anxious to have sex. In fact, I still almost never make the first move unless it is something my date indicates she wants. I believe you should date and get to know a person quite well before you begin having sex. Sex sorts of binds you to a person, and I don't want any such ties so shortly after my divorce. I had enough of possessiveness. It's a mistake to get into sex right away with your date.

"My idea of a woman I would find sexually attractive relates back to my wife's attitude toward sex—our lack of sexual compatibility. She thought of sex as dirty, and I thought of sex as a natural desire, as something to be enjoyed. I don't want to run into that attitude again. They don't have to go to bed with every man they meet, but the kind of woman I like is one who can enjoy sex; someone who can be adventurous in bed, someone who really enjoys sex and can be pretty free with her expressions. I think that it was lack of imagination more than anything else, and my ex-wife's filthy attitude about sex most of the time, that caused our problems.

"I have found out that there are some damned imaginative people out there, and that's worth a lot of chips. It's damn nice to feel that others find you attractive—sexually pleasing. It's good for my sense of self-worth. Not feeling that was a heavy handicap to me in my marriage. Sex is showing someone you care."

Roger began dating soon after his separation. He obviously had no guilt about dating, nor any psychological pain to prevent his becoming sexually active. He views sex as something to be enjoyed, a normal desire. George, whose wife initiated the divorce, is more typical, taking much longer to begin dating and thinking about sex. Peter, in his anxiety over his ability to perform, had a quick affair with a much younger woman. Many men admit that shortly after their wives told them they were no longer loved—feeling angry, betrayed, and stripped of their masculinity—they went to bars and picked up women for a one-night stand. These affairs usually were very unsatisfactory, but they did prove to a rejected man that he could still perform sexually, that a woman still found him sexually attractive. Rudolph had a one-night stand, and afterwards he conjectured, "I realized that picking up somebody in a bar at ten o'clock and laying them by midnight isn't something you take into your fifties. I woke up in the morning wondering who in the hell was this person in my bed. It's better getting sexual release from masturbation, and you don't have to worry about venereal disease."

There are notable differences between men who initiate divorce and men whose wives initiate it. Chuck, a forty-year-old artist whose decision to divorce was made jointly, has an interesting attitude toward dating, love, and sex. He has no guilt and no sexual fears, and he has his ex-wife's blessings. He says, "I thought after almost twenty years of marriage that I might have trouble dating, but I didn't. It was a little strange asking for a date the first time, but I wanted someone to talk to and to do something with. The first time I dated we went to stock car races and had a damn good time.

"Usually I take a date to some public place like a show or a ball game. I don't expect sex on the first date, and if she offers, I am a bit leery about it, with all the VD and herpes going around.

"Sometimes I am asked out when a gal needs an escort, and that is okay, too. Normally you just go out and feel each other out to see what each of you wants. Usually, I have sex on the second date. I have been out with ten different women and have gone to bed with all but one. And that one I just didn't trust. She was a tall, sexy woman, but I didn't trust her, and she probably thinks I am gay." Chuck feels some women want only a sexual relationship that lasts a short time with no commitment. He has found that women without a husband have sexual needs just as men do, and some women whose husbands have left them for younger women want to prove themselves to be sexually attractive to other men.

"Believe it or not, of the nine women I have bedded, eight of them are sterile, too. But most women expect that you are going to have a rubber to use," he said. "I am always surprised to find that most of these women had never enjoyed foreplay or an orgasm with their husbands—their husbands just stuck it in and that was that.

"I am going regularly with a woman now, and when I first met her she had never experienced an orgasm, and for a while I was thinking maybe she couldn't. But now I can keep her going for up to fifteen minutes. This is a lot of fun for her, and I enjoy it too, but I have no serious intentions about her, and she knows it. Sex is great, and I spend about forty-five minutes doing everything I can think of to warm her up until I have her screaming for intercourse. And like so many other women, she says, 'My husband never did this with me.' Then she asks, 'Did you do these things to your wife?' and I say, 'Yes, but she didn't like it.' And she can't believe it. But you just can't jump in the sack with a gal the first time you date her. I sure don't need to go to hookers for sex—there are enough women all for nothing."

It is clear that Chuck feels free to enjoy sex without any inhibitions or negative feelings. Recall Gordon, the clergyman-psychiatrist whose divorce was jointly decided upon when he was sixty-five and his wife was forty-five. He says, "I had some fear of my ability to perform sexually at the time of my divorce. My ex-wife, while not enjoying sex with me, constantly reminded me of the sexual prowess of her first husband. She didn't like this or that, and it was a very castrating experience for me. And then, when I did experience temporary impotence, she would ridicule me.

"So, shortly after my divorce, I began to date and found my sexual experiences very rewarding. I was a desirable man once again. My sexual needs sort of dwindled down after my first long-term sexual relationship ended by mutual consent. This affair began during the period of separation and ended just before the divorce was final. My wife had already left our place of residence, and I am sure she would not have objected to my dating even if she had known. I felt such a sense of freedom to enjoy life that I felt like thirty again."

Gordon's advice: "Don't get into any serious relationships just for sex as long as you have a good right hand. I really think masturbation can save more men from unhappy second marriages than anything else, if one can just get over the idea that there is something wrong with it. If the good Lord didn't want us to come that way, he wouldn't have made it possible. Now, masturbation isn't always the best way to relieve sexual tension, but every night you don't have a steak. Sometimes a hamburger is just as good.

"Frankly, I feel like Gertrude Stein, who said, 'A rose is a rose is a rose.' A come is a come is a come. Any ejaculation is good, and some are better than others. If you have no other choice, there is no point in being miserable. Just get out that old right hand, or left hand, or maybe both hands. Don't worry about that macho image. Of course, if you have an opportunity for other sexual expressions, use them, but when you don't, masturbate. When I awaken in the morning and feel the need to relieve myself, I masturbate. I can't very well call some dame up at six-thirty in the morning and ask her to hurry over, can I?"

Widowers

Interest in sex among widowers is generally lost for a period of time. The drive for sex varies for many reasons, including the age of the widower, satisfaction with the marital relationship, and the type of death. Widowers often find it difficult to approach a woman for sex. However, men whose wives die unexpectantly, as in the case of suicide, seem to develop a more intense need for sex in the early stages of bereavement. Masturbation is a satisfactory means to meet their sexual needs, as it is for divorced men.

The primary reason widowed men begin to date and return to the coupled world is a need for companionship—someone just to talk with, to have dinner with, to fill the void brought about by the loneliness of being without a wife. Their advice generally is: "The sooner you decide to date, the better. Be sure to date a variety of women. It's a matter of starting a new life."

Whether a widower waits three months or a year after his wife dies to begin casual dating, it is difficult to take that first plunge. "You probably haven't had to ask for a date for years, and you are out of practice, fearful to make that first phone call," is a typical comment. For some, casual dating is initially pleasant. Michael, thirty-one, says, "I guess it was six months before I really felt like having some fun. It was then that I began dating. I would be less than honest if I didn't say that I was physically attracted to women, and I spend considerable time pursuing those interests, good, bad, or indifferent.

"At first, I was not interested in any long-term relationship. Friends were always arranging for me to meet women, and I enjoyed this casual dating. I had no problem with dating. I made the mistake of trying the bar scene shortly after my wife died when I had a sudden wild need for sex. But it wasn't my style and will never be, and I don't recommend it. I decided picking up a gal at a bar was not for me, and now, with venereal diseases in epidemic proportions, it is particularly wise to know the gal well before having a sexual relationship. But I did meet a lot of nice people, and I have dated everybody, small, large, old, young. Eventually I developed a more than casual relationship that lasted for a period of a year. I found I couldn't handle a one-night affair and that the more long-term affair was most comfortable for me."

Michael found casual dating pleasant and easy to handle. However, to a great extent, success with dating depends on many factors, including one's attitude toward a new relationship. Also, age makes a difference. Younger men begin dating much sooner after the death of their wives than older men. Mark, thirty-six, whose wife died after a short illness, dated a good friend of his wife's two months after the wife's death. "But," he says, "the first time I dated someone new to me was in about a year. My wife's friend had been a widow for quite some time, and we both needed companionship. But this relationship developed much more quickly than I had expected and became too intense too soon.

"The funny thing about this is that I was well aware how lonely and vulnerable a person is during the first year or so after his wife dies. You may not think you are lonely, but you are, and this can lead into something you don't intend because you are so hungry for companionship and affection. I really thought that I was entering into a lasting relationship.

"This went on for six months until one day all of a sudden I realized that I didn't need her. It was an uplifting experience, knowing I didn't have to depend on anyone. I can do anything I want to do! You see, I had become too dependent on her, so our relationship ended. I felt horrible about it because it was very painful for her. I had never done that before to anyone, and it hurt. But I realized if I didn't make the break, the agony would just be prolonged. I think it was a maturing process on my part. I realize we should not get serious with a person early in the dating game. Keep it casual. Date several girls at least before settling for a longer-term relationship."

Attitude and how a man defines his situation probably are more important than age in determining success in establishing new relationships. Karl, for example, felt that life was over for him when his wife of twenty-four years died. He says, "I loved my wife dearly and believed that I was incapable of finding anyone else I would want to marry.

"I suppose I thought I might marry some day. Most men have the capacity for loving more than one wife. This is an obvious fact that I didn't fully comprehend when I was living through those terrible days of loneliness."

At age fifty-seven, Earl found casual dating very easy. He says, "I was widowed less than two months when I was invited to a party by some matchmaking friends, and I was dating soon after. I joined an organization for widowed persons. I am a happy person, so it did not take me long to find dating partners." Earl had another advantage— unlike Karl, he never felt that there is a once-in-a-lifetime romance. He always thought he could have been happily married to a different woman even though he loved his wife and felt lucky to have been married to her.

Each man defines his situation according to his own personal needs and feelings. Many widowers find casual dating difficult because they initially try to recapture the same deep feelings with the same type of person as their first wife.

Charles, a widower in his forties, had different problems. He says, "At my age and with five young children, it was very difficult for me to find dating partners. Not only did I have baby-sitting problems, but I found that women shy away from entanglements with men who have young children. Also, I hesitated to date because I really didn't know how or where to begin or how my children would react."

Ralph, at seventy-seven, found that children inhibited his dating, too, but in a different way. He says, "My two daughters were married with families themselves when my wife died, and yet they seemed very resentful at the thought of their father even thinking about women and dating. They would tell me I was too old, or I should wait a while. But at seventy-seven, I didn't have much time. If I was going to spend two or three years looking for a woman, I might as well forget it."

When Ralph first decided to date a woman he had known from church, his children's resentment surfaced. "I was financially well off and very well known in our community, and lots of widows hinted that they would like a date," Ralph said. "But I was interested in finding a woman who would become my wife—no more casual dating for me. I was lonesome and unhappy without someone to share my life. I believed that dating would help ease my pain, and I moved along very rapidly toward marriage. I wasn't going to worry about what my children thought, either. I have a life to lead, and they have theirs."

Ralph says, "Friends can be a wonderful help in finding a woman—they know you pretty well, and they have your welfare in mind. One Friday night a couple that my wife and I used to chum around with invited me to the country club for a fish fry. Once we got there, my friends pointed out a lady whom I had known for several years, but I did not know she was widowed, too. They told me to go over and talk to her, and that started our courtship. I called her for a date, and we just seemed to get along well. She was happy, and we both liked to have good times. I was lonesome, and then all of a sudden my life was filled with happiness again."

Ralph moved rapidly from dating to thoughts of marriage. He felt the urgency of time because of his age. His matchmaking friends had been interested in finding him another wife, and he reacted to this with appreciation rather than with indifference or resentment. He did not experience the "she cannot be replaced" feeling, which tends to inhibit a man from dating and eventually remarrying. This man had no guilt feelings about his desire for the companionship and love of another woman.

Several widowers say they feel as though they are cheating when they first begin to think of dating. Yet Samuel thinks there is no reason to feel this way: "My wife is dead, and when I had reached the limits of my grief, I knew very well I had to have a woman to love." Like most widowers, he began to think about companionship right after his wife died, knowing he would never survive alone. Samuel feels a widower should never think he is cheating on his wife when he starts dating again. He concludes, "The relationship with my wife was separate and something special, and will be remembered as such. But the relationship has ended, and it does not prevent my establishing another meaningful one."

It is clear that widowers begin dating to fill a terrible void in their lives. They miss the company of a woman. And eventually sex becomes an important issue. Often it is when the need arises for a sexual relationship that men develop deep, serious conflicts about their sexuality. It is one thing to date, but the desire for intimacy, for sexual release, is something else. Mark, for example, says, "I did not feel guilty when I first began dating, but when I began to get sexually involved with the woman I intended to marry, I felt a great deal of guilt. Probably because I saw a lot of good qualities in her that my wife never had. It is a very guilty feeling thinking you have found someone so much better in many ways than who you had in your first marriage. This was hard to cope with."

How a man perceives his previous marital relationship seems to be an important factor in how he resolves his need for a sexual relationship. Mark, for example, says, "Marriage had a lot of very big highs and a lot of very big lows. My wife went through a lot of sickness throughout our marriage. When she felt well, we had lots of good times. But when she was sick and depressed, it was horrible. She was very explosive, demanding, not compromising, inflexible. But she did have a good sense of humor, and we did have our fun times. As I said before, the guilt I felt is because I found a prospective wife with so many better qualities. But I didn't feel more guilt, probably because there were so many bad feelings between my wife and me."

Men with strong guilt feelings run the risk of sexual dysfunction. David, for example, was shocked to discover that he was impotent. It was three years after his wife's death before he attempted to have sexual intercourse, because he always felt so guilty about wanting sex. Eventually he encountered a widow he had known for years, who invited him to her apartment for a drink. "She was in as much need for sexual release as I was," he recalls. "We went to bed only to the embarrassment of us both. I could not get an erection. So tormented was I at the thought of being impotent that I wouldn't even consider dating for several months."

Then David met a lovely woman at a party who, after a few dates, began to arouse sexual feelings in him. "We would have beautiful evenings in each other's arms kissing and petting," he says. "But I could not bring myself to chance a failure in sexual intercourse. I knew she loved me, for she was understanding of my plight and tried to lessen my embarrassment. We joined in mutual masturbation to achieve a sexual release, something we continued to do. Finally one evening it happened. I was no longer impotent. We regularly had sexual relations, although periodically I would go through a brief period of impotence when a feeling of guilt would return."

Most men whose wives die after an illness find it very difficult to approach a woman for sex, and it usually takes six months to a year before their sex drive returns.

Greg, a sixty-year-old pastor whose wife died of cancer, says he had a terrible time even getting up courage to ask the woman he was very attracted to for that first date. About his marital relationship, he says: "My wife was always somewhat infrequent in her own intensity regarding sexual needs. Several weeks would pass between our having intercourse. Now for me, that was not enough, so I would masturbate. That's the only outlet I used other than inter-course with my wife on those infrequent occasions. Neither my wife nor I had any moral qualms about masturbation."

Greg says he and his wife had a good understanding early in their marriage about about their sexual needs. He says he loved his wife very much and never pushed sex on her. He understood and respected her needs, and she understood his intense sexual needs that had to be released at times through masturbation.

"After my wife's death my sexuality was repressed for several months," he says. "I just didn't think about sex. I'm not one who could be promiscuous. I have a phobia about personal cleanliness, and unless I knew a person well I couldn't touch her. I knew I would really have to care for a woman very much before wanting sex with her.

"I didn't turn to masturbation at first, and I used to have wet dreams. I can remember thinking, 'What is the cleaning lady going to think about these messy sheets?' When I resumed masturbation, this problem ended.

"Virginia told me many times she would want me to be happy with another woman if she died first. Now I have found a very beautiful woman who loves me and desires me as much as I do her, but it took me three years to arrive at this state of euphoria."

A man whose wife dies unexpectedly is as likely to find it difficult to approach a woman for sex as a man whose wife died after an illness, depending, again, upon how they perceived their marital life. Frank, age fifty-nine, lost his wife suddenly when she suffered an acute heart attack. He says, "We had a perfect and ideal marriage. We just agreed on so many things. Sure we argued, but we would always settle things to our mutual satisfaction. Until my illness, which left me partially impotent, we had a very sensuous, loving, sexual relationship.

"Even after two years, I can't think of replacing her in my life. But I am not being morbid. I have made many changes in my house with some new decorative ideas—it looks more masculine now. As for women, they seem to find me attractive, and I have financial means since I am a physician. Yet, I feel no need to initiate a date. Oh, I could have lots of dates—I get so many calls—and I probably have made an ass out of myself with the dumb excuses I use to get out of the invitations. My wife and I had such a beautiful relationship I am not ready for another one, and I couldn't think of having sex."

However, many men whose wives committed suicide felt an extraordinary strong urge for sex shortly afterward. Craig, a fifty-year-old businessman tells of his wild, uncontrollable needs: "Those months after her death, I began to satisfy my sexual needs with various women. This promiscuity lasted for a couple of months before this wild urge settled down. Perhaps it was my anger at my wife, maybe a terrible sense of rejection. Did I want to get back at her?"

Craig recalls that in the beginning of his marriage their sex life was fair. His wife never responded with the abandonment he wished for, and after four children and six miscarriages in eight years, she began to withdraw from him out of fear of another pregnancy. Her religious faith would only allow the rhythm method of birth control, and she knew that did not work. "I know we were not all that happy in our marriage, but she never gave me the idea that it was bad enough for her to commit suicide," he says. "Maybe it was her menopause, but who can say? She certainly did not enjoy sex. I think I spent half of the later years of our marriage sleeping on the sofa in our living room. She would use any excuse to get angry at me so that she could shut me out of our bedroom.

"I was just sick about everything. I was upset with myself that I hadn't realized how bad the situation really was. I just remember the great emptiness, and I thought it was a dirty deal. I was angry that she did this to our family. And I had guilt. It must be my fault that she was unhappy enough to take her own life. I tried to sublimate my doubts, my anger, my guilt through sex.

"I was a wreck. I was crying around the house. And yet, I had this tremendous desire to have a woman—to prove that I was still attractive to women—to drown out that terrible feeling of rejection I got from thinking how little my wife had cared for me. And I didn't feel guilty one little bit over this strong, intense sexual need. But I soon found that sex was not the answer. And then the impotence hit me. I went from extreme sex drive to no drive at all—from tremendous desire, to no desire.

"My God, I dated more damn women trying to find someone to turn me on!" Craig says. "I sought professional help to understand the many feelings I had about my situation—guilt, anger, resentment, and sadness. Finally my impotence corrected itself, but it still will recur now and then. Though I understand occasional impotence is normal, it occurs at the most inopportune times—and that's a hell of an embarrassing moment."

For widowers especially, emotions have a great deal of control over the ability to function sexually. Guilt feelings very often keep them from recognizing and fulfilling sexual needs. But a conscious attempt to sublimate sexual needs may result in impotence.

Many middle-aged men become impotent following the death of their wives. For most, this is temporary, a normal lack of desire for sex felt immediately after the death of a wife. For others, impotence after several months of sexual inactivity becomes a problem.

In this sense, Walter was fortunate—a few months following his wife's death he received a phone call from a psychotherapist and good friend inquiring how he was doing. She asked Walter if he had found someone to sleep with, and he replied that he had not, nor did he wish to. She asked him if he had been masturbating, and he replied in all honesty that he had not—that he was having a difficult time and simply didn't have any sexual feelings.

He says "I was stunned when she asked me to promise that I would masturbate before I went to sleep that night. In her very gentle way she explained to me that men who don't remain sexually active *may* become impotent. I have become very appreciative of her advice. I did masturbate whenever the need arose, and when I did meet a woman with whom I desired sex, whether masturbating helped or not, I was able to perform magnificently!"

Long-term abstinence may make it difficult for a man to think in terms of becoming active sexually again. There is a great deal of evidence to indicate that a man's sexual problems are primarily a matter of mind rather than physical disability. It is for this reason that I would suggest to a widower having difficulties with sex to seek counseling.

Depression is a common cause of impotence, and it is normal not to be able to function in this condition. However, since physical problems may also be present, it is always a good idea first to have a physical examination. Once such possibilities are eliminated, as they will be in about 90 percent of the cases, one then might take a more realistic look at his expectations. For example, a man of sixty will have less stamina for sex than a man of thirty—his erection may not be as firm at sixty but even so, impotence is seldom a matter of aging. What a man may lose in plain stamina he may gain in qualities that make him a better lover, such as patience and tenderness. Also, research indicates that while an older man may take longer to get an erection, the erection lasts longer and can provide increased satisfaction for his partner.

Knowing that impotence is primarily a matter of mind and that like all other parts of the body, the sex organs function best with regular use, newly single men should be encouraged to seek professional help if impotence continues beyond a reasonable length of time. It is important to know that most cases of impotence can be cured if a man has the will to try.

Not being sure of what is expected in the area of sex also troubles some men. Walter comments, "I am basically shy with women, and when attracted to a woman, I simply can't say, 'Let's go make love.' One evening I was with a lovely lady who was divorced. We talked about the problems of being alone. And to my pleasant surprise this truly great lady asked if I would like to go to bed with her.

"It's not the words one uses that are the most important in extending an invitation to go to bed; it's the feeling that one conveys," says Walter. "I was always afraid I would offend someone. Had I known that many women are as fully sexual as I am, I would not have worried. Sex among loving friends is great."

This, of course, is Walter's personal opinion about sex before marriage. But it appears he has a great deal of support for his point of view. "When two adults enjoy each other and desire sex together, why wait until marriage? Surely we don't have to worry about virginity, and we men aren't so inexperienced and irresponsible that we would be indiscreet or otherwise hurt the woman with whom we make love."

We have discussed the difficulty that many men have in finding dates, but this is not true for all formerly married men. Walter found it delightful that women made their availability known to him. He says, "Most men really are not offended if they receive an invitation to go to bed, and just as it is easy for a woman to decline, I have learned to say, 'I couldn't possibly do that, for if I did, I'm afraid you'd lose all respect for me!' I have yet to meet a woman who didn't laugh."

Probably the greatest help for men in coping with sexual frustration comes from the realization that most people don't expect formerly married persons to quit being sexual at the loss of their spouses. Understanding this, the widowed and divorced need not be so concerned about other people's opinions. Walter says, "When people ask me now if I engaged in sexual intercourse during the time I was a widower, I say, 'Of course.' If people can't accept my response, they shouldn't ask. Although I am a very conservative person, I now find it pointless to lie. *Normal* people expect other normal people to respond sexually. Frankly, the people I wonder about are those who don't."

That's true, of course, up to a certain age, but when a person reaches the age of sixty or older, our society seems to consider him over the hill as far as sex is concerned. Ralph, an elderly widower, says, "I know my daughters were plain embarrassed at the thought of their father still being interested in sex.

"I also think a lot of elderly people think they can't or shouldn't have a sex life. They really miss out on a lot of life's pleasures, and it's much harder to get along together when you can't be intimate. I've always found that having sex makes me much easier to get along with. It's a special problem when one person craves sex, and the other spouse doesn't. I'm glad that I still have a good craving for sex. Keeps me young!"

It is a pity so little is known about the sexual activity and attitudes of older people. There are many misconceptions about the role of sex in the lives of older people in our society, the greatest being that in the later stages of life sexual activity ceases.

People should realize that aging is a gradual process, not something that happens when a person reaches a certain birthday. Aging involves a person's lessened physical vigor, but it is when a person begins to *feel* old, sometimes long before he has actually aged physiologically, that he actually becomes old. As Samuel says, "Having sex together at any age is good—it makes you feel loved."

Many widowers hope dating will ultimately lead to love and marriage, but many, because of guilt or loyalty, cannot separate themselves emotionally from their deceased wife. Those who believe there is no replacement for their one-and-only love may find happiness in their life as a single person. But for others, friendship, affection, and love give meaning to their lives and can lessen that terrible loneliness that affects everyone who has lost a loved one.

Summary

Divorced men begin dating and having sexual relationships sooner than widowers, and with less guilt than widowers. There are many parallels in the attitudes expressed by both categories of men regarding dating and sexuality. Most advise getting involved in living as soon as possible. Find people to talk to, and find women to date through groups, the work place, or community activities or organizations. Dating should be casual at first.

Probably the greatest help in coping with sexual frustration comes from the realization that most people do not expect a man to quit being sexual after the loss of his wife. Granted, society often expects that a divorced person will be enjoying a sexual relationship very shortly after the separation. On the other hand, widowed persons may be expected to wait for "that sensible year" before dating. The most reasonable thing to do is begin circulating as soon as you feel the need for female companionship. Never mind what other people might think. Put your own needs first. This is not being selfish. It is a sign of mature love, so necessary if you are to survive a broken relationship. Mature love means being capable of loving yourself for being who you are. If you develop a strong sense of self-love, then when your wife tells you she no longer loves you, your self-image won't be completely shattered, because you are still a worthwhile, lovable person in your own image. It is the man who feels completely unworthy and unloved who is compelled to prove he is still attractive to women. Beware the hazards of becoming involved too quickly in a "heavy" relationship, or in becoming sexually promiscuous.

In chapter seven we turn to companionship, love, a sexual relationship, and happiness the "second time around."

7

Thoughts of Remarriage

JUST as there are differences between the two types of newly single men when it comes to fulfilling needs for love and sex, so, too, are there differences on the issue of remarriage.

Many divorced men are positive about remarrying eventually, saying they don't want to end their lives alone. Men who have been divorced for less than two years tend to be more skeptical about marriage than those who have been divorced longer.

Widowers, on the other hand, find different paths to healing and returning to a reasonably happy life. For some the path includes remarriage, about which they generally feel no guilt, but others enjoy their new freedom and choose to remain single. Age is often a factor. Younger men with children in their care typically feel pressured into remarriage. Older widowers often find comfort through moving in with their children or into a retirement community where they often become quite active.

Divorced Men

While statistics suggest a high rate of remarriage among the divorced, some exhibit a great deal of trepidation about it. Many factors enter into a man's decision to remarry or not: How long he has been divorced, the intensity of negative emotions that accompanied the divorce, the resources available to help him cope with and work through the grief process, his financial situation, and his child custody arrangements. One of the biggest factors is the time element. Let's begin with comments from a man who is still in the process of divorce, conclude with a man who took seventeen years to consider remarriage, and discuss several men who are "in between."

Samuel, at age fifty-two, has just recently filed for divorce. "I may have a fantasy about maybe someday establishing a real deep meaningful relationship with another person. But I am a lot more appreciative about how bloody hard it is to get out of a marriage, how expensive it can be. Even if I felt a commitment toward marriage again, I would be more worried about getting married the second time than I was the first time. I don't have the feeling of 'never again,' but it's a pretty remote question at the present time.

"I wouldn't be interested in marrying anyone who wasn't an autonomous person. I certainly would not want another wife dependent upon me for her being, meaning, existence. Right now I have three good reasons why I don't have positive thoughts toward remarriage. One, I don't want the responsibility; two, I don't think it would be fun; and three, I am not sure marriage can give me the happiness I desire. When I was young, there was a whole set of fantasies about marriage—Prince Charming, Princess Charming, marrying, and living happily ever after. Maybe my expectation of marriage and what commitment it would provide for me were unrealistic. Right now I cannot contemplate remarriage with the thoughts of my miserable marriage so fresh in my mind."

Ralph's second wife initiated their divorce about six months ago. He, too, still has not had time to sort out his feelings. "I am really mixed up on the question of remarriage. I don't know if I would ever want to remarry. I have really only dated twice on a steady basis, and I broke those relationships off. I just am not ready for that kind of involvement, and I know I won't be for quite a long time. Freedom is great. I felt too close to the first woman I dated, and what I really wanted was to be free to date others, but she could not understand this, nor could several other women I dated. They would not accept me on a basis where I was also free to date others, so I had to break off the relationships. It was hard because they were lovely ladies, but I am not ready for an exclusive relationship. It made me resentful. The difficulty is that you like to have friends, but women so often get very demanding of you."

Roger had a strong desire to remain single for quite a while before his first marriage, and now when he thinks of the kind of headaches he endured when he was married, he is unsure. "When you are single and lonely, you pick up the phone and talk to friends. And if you want to be alone, you can. When you are married, and you want to be alone, you can't. At least, my wife refused to give me any privacy. Right now, I don't really want to think about remarriage. I have three young children, and they are getting my full attention. I may not remarry until my children are grown—from my own experience, I don't want my children to live with a stepmother." Roger had a very unhappy marriage and a difficult divorce, and coupled with the short time since his separation, one can easily understand his reticence regarding remarriage.

Jim has been divorced for a year, after a bitter experience when his wife left him for a lesbian relationship. He says emphatically, "I will not remarry. My feelings right now are that there is absolutely no reason for marriage except for the purpose of having children. And I don't ever intend to have any more children (I had a vasectomy to please my wife); therefore, there's no reason for me to get married.

"Now, I am not saying that I may not want a long-term relationship, but without the marriage certificate. If one or the other feels our relationship is no longer suitable, I want no constraints on us. I never want to go through what I did when my wife asked me to leave. I like an independent women who can get along on her own. I want her to have a career of her own and a life apart from me. I don't want to be involved again with somebody who is dependent upon me."

Jim believes that communication, which he and his wife did not have, is really the key to a happy marriage. "It's important to find someone who expresses love the way you want to be loved and perceives love the way you do," he says. "When there is conflict in the way love is perceived by two people, the relationship can become very destructive and very frustrating. I have always had a hard time communicating my thoughts, and this was probably my contribution to the break-up of my marriage. If my wife had known what I wanted, and if I had known what was wrong in her mind, we might have dealt more adequately with the stress in our relationship."

Samuel, Roger, and Jim all carry emotional scars which are too recent for them to want to remarry, and two of them found their wives' dependency deplorable. Dependency is also an issue for George, who, at the age of forty-nine, was divorced by his wife two years ago. He, on the other hand, would like to marry some day, and is presently seeing a psychiatrist to help sort out his feelings. He says, "I need help to change some of my attitudes that developed in my first marriage. I am a bit scared. I guess I don't have too positive an attitude toward marriage. Actually, I have never seen what I would call a really happy marriage. Most marriages in my age group seem to continue not because the people wish them to continue on or are enjoying them, but because it is the thing to do.

"And this is the thing that stops me from remarrying. I am presently in a very satisfactory relationship. We see each other about every day, and yet she has her life and I have mine separately. We go on trips and vacations together, and have a good sex life. We are both satisfied with this arrangement, partly for financial considerations. I have substantial child support payments, and it scares me to think of taking on her financial problems along with mine. I also don't want to make another mistake in marriage, and I am getting to value my independence. I am thoroughly enjoying our relationship, but I don't want to give up my independence or take on additional responsibilities." After two years George has developed a fairly positive attitude toward remarriage. Still, he is reluctant to marry again and prefers for now a long-term relationship where each partner maintains his or her own household.

Gerry initiated his divorce three years ago and is now living with a woman associated with his profession. He says, "I wholeheartedly agree that I want to be married. I don't however, like that term right now because it's tied too much with the past. Marriage to me means being tied down or tied to, and I don't like that because I have been stifled by an overly dependent woman for seventeen years.

"I think that marriage means in our society a final commitment, and even though Sarah and I are both monogamously oriented and don't fool around on the side, we still have an open-ended relationship, which means a way out. I was under the illusion that I would be married again within two years. I am finding now that after three years I still have a long way to go to become healthy, to become okay enough to get into a total commitment.

"I surely don't want to end up my life alone. It will be that need for companionship, a sexual relationship, to be loved totally, that will carry me into another marriage. But first I have to develop a good self-image. I have to be happy with my own life. I have to cut the ties with the past, and I've got to live for today. Then I may be ready for marriage again."

Men who have been divorced for longer periods of time tend to have a more positive view toward remarriage. Warren was divorced by his wife seven years ago. "If I think about remarriage from a rational or intellectualized point of view, I don't think my enjoyment of my independence would be a problem, because there are women who feel the same way.

"There are a lot of women out there who appear to want to preserve their independence and might respect my independence, and it's quite conceivable that I would find someone like that who I could love totally, and then there would be only minor problems or adjustments. It's not that I feel that any marriage as such is threatening to me—it's the question, can I find the person I fit with? It's also not that I don't want to take on the responsibilities of marriage—and I don't think of marriage as meaning a restriction on freedom, necessarily. To the extent that I don't feel the need to remarry, I don't think that I look at remarriage as an imposition or burden on my life. It's because I think I see how difficult it is to really achieve a good marriage—not impossible, but difficult.

"I know of some wonderful marriages, so I know it is possible. It can be done, but it has to be approached with caution. But when you have had my experience with marriage, when do you trust your own feelings again? How could we have been so wrong? What went wrong?"

Daniel, age forty-two, is perhaps at the extreme end of this spectrum of feelings about remarriage. Seventeen years after his divorce, he says this: "I am planning to marry within the year. The primary reason for not marrying sooner was that I wanted to prove myself with my research. I have been a workaholic, devoting most of my time to my work, which gave me little time for thinking of marriage. I have had a few long-term relationships, and many platonic relationships with female colleagues, so my life has not been devoid of affection and sex. I enjoy being single. My research was for me truth, beauty, and love all wrapped into one. Anyone entering my life until my project was completed would have been an intruder, an annoyance, a nuisance.

"Now I think I am ready to celebrate the fact of life that I need love, sex, and marriage in my life every day. I am ready, and I am going to help myself to the happiness I think I will find married to the woman I love."

As these men indicate, remarriage is something that requires time and careful consideration. However, many divorced men enjoy their newly found freedom and intend to maintain it for a variety of reasons. Mark, who has custody of his young children, says, "It would be great to be loved and to love someone, but it will take a long time for me to decide to marry again. And there are the children to consider. I really enjoy them, but in a few years they will become independent and leave. I know that is coming, and I wonder if I will want to be alone. I have learned many things about caring for a home and children, and will be much more appreciative of these things the next time around. The only reason for *not* getting married is the risk of being hurt again. I wouldn't want a wife who would come in and try to take over my children. I would want a wife, not a mother for my children. Because of the children, I will not rush into marriage. We are getting along very well. And I am enjoying my freedom as a single-again man."

Bob was sixty-five when he and his wife jointly decided upon a divorce. He says, "I may be self-centered, but I am enjoying my freedom to come and go, no questions asked, so much that I am sure I will never remarry. I have several platonic relationships with women friends, and if I want sex, it is for hire. Prostitutes are safer than pick-ups. I am never lonely. I have so many activities—golf, sailing, playing cards, travel—that my life is full. In addition, I have a very loving set of children and grandchildren who give me an ample dose of attention, love, and affection and the sense of being important. Remarriage? No need for my sense of well-being."

Dean, a thirty-five-year-old high school teacher whose divorce was accomplished by mutual agreement has a positive attitude toward remarriage. Two years after his divorce he began dating a colleague. He says: "After ten years of marriage my ex-wife and I were strangers. We had our son in common and that was all. I think I was more to blame than she for our drifting apart. I am a workaholic and always put my work ahead of her needs. She developed her own outside interests, so we really saw little of each other. She was never interested in sex, and after our son was born she stopped sleeping with me.

"Now I have met Jean, and I know she is the right person for me. She has a kind, happy disposition—a personality that will blend with mine. I can get very angry, and she helps me express my feelings instead of causing me to hold my emotions inside. She is teaching me by her example how to communicate openly and honestly." Dean likes it that he and Jean can talk about anything— quite a change from what he experienced in his first marriage, in which he says it was safer to keep still than to say what was on his mind. Their incomes are about equal, and Jean intends to continue teaching, so that his financial support of his son will not put any undue strain on their marriage. He says, "She is a very sexy lady and makes me glad I'm a man, as the saying goes.

"We want to have children, and we see no problem between parenting and continuing our teaching careers. Jean will be a marvelous homemaker, and we want to share this role. Since we have been dating we have been included in the 'coupled world,' much to our enjoyment. Wedding bells will ring for us in two months.

"We have invited my ex-wife and her boyfriend to our wedding, and they have accepted. It's funny, but now my ex-wife and I can talk to each other. We can be friends, and this is okay with Jean."

David, a forty-six-year-old college professor, was also divorced by mutual consent. Recently he took his ex-wife out for lunch to celebrate her birthday. His father-in-law, a widower, is a frequent visitor in David's home. After four years of living as a fun-loving bachelor, David has decided he wants to marry again. He says, "I'm tired of the singles crowd, I'm tired of keeping house by myself, I'm tired of masturbating for sexual release, or sleeping with casual friends. I want a home with a wife and children. Now I have found Mary, a widow with two children, who feels the same sense of loss without a spouse. She is a superb hostess and a lady of means. When we marry I plan to move into her home. We know there may be problems for me in relating to the children, but since we communicate very openly with each other and with her ten-year-old son and her twelve-year-old daughter, I think the problems will be minimized. In addition to fulfilling my wish for a family, we are also very sexually compatible. That was one of my big fears—not being able to enjoy sex on a regular basis."

To summarize, there are a variety of reasons why divorced men consider remarriage: for companionship, for sex with love, for fear of not being able to have sex on a regular basis, to re-establish themselves in a couples' world, to grow emotionally and spiritually, to have a homemaker, to be with someone who is open with her feelings, and to have mutual support.

Reasons why divorced men do not want to remarry include: enjoyment of independence and freedom, not wanting responsibility of marriage again (the most frequent reason), and a lingering attachment to their ex-wives. For men with children in their custody, economic obligation is the chief reason, along with not wanting to become involved in stepparenting. A typical response, from a man divorced for nine years, is, "I'm not thinking of marriage until my children are independent. Actually, I can't afford a second marriage. My children come first. They have suffered enough disruption in their lives from the divorce."

There seems to be a consensus on what is necessary for a happy marriage: the right partner (one with a kind, friendly disposition), an ability to communicate openly and honestly with each other, financial security, and some acceptance by family and friends.

Widowers

How soon does a widowed man remarry, if at all? That depends upon how soon and how well he adjusted to the many facets of being single again and to a considerable extent on his age. Most widowers seem amenable to the idea of remarriage. For some, it is the clearest path to happiness.

Tom is happily married again three years after his wife's death. "But," he cautions, "choosing a second wife is a precarious situation. You must look for similarities in values, habits, and customs, because in a remarriage differences can become ten times more problematic than in a first marriage. You have to have a strong commitment to the person you are going to marry. She's the one you have really been looking for. You must love her so deeply that you feel certain you will take whatever comes—and you had better feel that way, because difficult situations are going to come up. If you can't handle these situations together, then your relationship will just fall apart. You can't just say, 'Well, she's a good cook, and she will take good care of my children, and I think we will get along okay.' You have to be sure of the relationship and, and this takes time."

Tom also cautions that a man had better not jump in as a rebound to grief. "If he thinks he must get somebody in his house—in his bed—as soon as possible, he's in for problems. He may marry someone he doesn't even love. So timing is an important issue. If a man can sit back and live with himself for a year or two, I don't think he will make the mistake of a rebound marriage."

Tom believes people put on a facade, and it is hard sometimes to tell what a person is really like. He suggests spending time in evaluating a new relationship—being together in various circumstances such as during a crisis, some mistake the one or the other makes, or an unhappy experience—not just on dates, when both people have their best foot forward.

Tom said someone considering remarriage should definitely make sure it is with a person he can spend the rest of his life with and whom he can favorably compare to his first wife. "I know comparisons are unfair," he says, "but whether you admit it to yourself or not, you are going to compare this woman to the wife you lived with for so many years. And if she doesn't stack up and there are too many negatives, hey, that's not going to last. Fortunately, my new wife is much more compatible to my needs than was my first wife.

"Most of this is just common sense. I do realize that under emotional stress people do silly things, but if we would just use the common sense that God gave us, and sit back for awhile and say, 'Wait a minute, don't be in such a rush,' a widower could save himself the anguish of a marriage that didn't last. At least let's use the same sense we would use in a business deal or in buying a new car."

While many widowers find happiness through a remarriage, others enjoy their newly found freedom and intend to maintain it for a variety of reasons. Samuel, after four years of being widowed, feels he has learned to cope very well as a bachelor. He says he has finally gotten the hang of living alone. I have a pleasant house, and I am comfortable, and there are times when I just like to be by myself.

"My problem with thinking about marriage is my age," he said. "I am sixty-eight and I don't know how many more productive years I would have to offer a woman. I don't expect to exit from this earth in the near future, for I am very healthy. But at the same time, if you marry a gal, you expect to offer her a modicum of security and perhaps something to look forward to in improvement of her situation. And that may not be in the cards. I've progressed in my work as far as I can go, and I just don't know what I could offer anybody. I am programmed to think that a man should be the provider, and I could not easily accept being provided for by a wife.

"I have no guilt feelings about getting married again. I faced my guilt feelings when I thought to myself, 'Hey, Marion would be the first one to tell me that she's gone and I'm still alive and that we had a fine life and I have nothing to regret or be ashamed of, so why not?' The fact is that my religious beliefs allow me to think that Marion is still close, and I talk to her quite frequently. It's a little one-sided, but I have a feeling I'm getting answers. All in all, I have little need for a woman in my life. I am content as things are. Not that I don't enjoy several platonic relationships with the opposite sex."

Samuel is enjoying his newly found freedom. He is older and has no responsibility for children. He is very mobile and wants to remain free to come and go as he pleases with no marital strings attached.

Older widowers such as Samuel may be content with happy memories. On the other hand, a widower may have had such an uncomfortable first marriage that it would take much convincing for him to risk marriage again.

Jake, a fifty-year-old construction engineer, had experienced a "living hell" for twenty-five years of his married life. "Marry again, you ask—never," he says. "I married Stella because she told me I was the father of her unborn child. I expected that we could make things work, but I did not reckon with her nasty disposition. As time went on she became more domineering, and unless she had her way, life was a terror for me and our three children. For the last ten years of her life she became an alcoholic, but would not admit her addiction. She was a sloppy housekeeper, and sex was nonexistent after our last child was born. Nothing I ever did pleased her, and she always compared me negatively with her family. I wonder why I didn't divorce her. Yet when the children were still home, I wouldn't break up our home. And, being a practicing Catholic, I felt obligated to stay in the marriage no matter what.

"Her death was sudden—a heart attack while she was in a fit of rage. Her last words to me were: 'You goddamn bastard.' I had to put on a bit of an act at the wake and funeral for the benefit of her family, and one never wants to see a person die at a fairly young age.

"Actually, I had to do most of the household chores, so nothing has changed much around the house except the disruptions caused by my wife's drinking and nasty disposition.

"I don't miss her. I don't feel guilty for enjoying the tranquility of my life. Maybe someday I might consider remarriage, but I strongly doubt I will ever want to run the risk of an unhappy marriage again."

The context in which older and younger widowers consider the decision to remarry can be very different. Once an elderly widower gets through the stage of severe grief and loneliness, societal and family pressures often support his remaining single. He isn't expected to have a sex drive, and even if he does, chances are he has learned to sublimate these feelings because "old men aren't supposed to feel this way." His children are grown and don't need a mother. In fact, often they would rather not have him remarry, for this might threaten their expected inheritance!

For example, Emil, a seventy-eight-year-old retired plant manager, was ridiculed by his fifty-year-old daughter when he expressed an interest in a widowed neighbor. He says, "My daughter told me in no uncertain terms that I was too old to be interested in other women and that if I really loved Mother I wouldn't be thinking about dating. Then she 'lowered the boom' by telling me the whole family had decided they wouldn't let some woman get her hands on my money—it belonged to them after I died!

"I paid them no attention and am dating my neighbor. She is sixty-five, well-fixed financially, and lots of fun to be with, and we have an enjoyable sexual relationship. That would really turn my kids off! She is not interested in remarriage, but in time, who knows?"

Loneliness may be abated for an older man if he moves in with his children or to a retirement community. Of course, this choice depends upon the kind of hospitality and care he receives. Churches and various social and government agencies provide many activities for the older man who seeks companionship. Free community meal service, parties, card clubs, and the like are also provided for the elderly. An elderly widower who wants to remain single usually finds support for his decision in social acceptance, and he is provided with opportunities to interact with other elderly singles.

Alex, an eighty-five-year-old retired physician, is enjoying life in a retirement community since his wife died. He lives in a two-bedroom condominium, tastefully furnished for him by his children. He seems very contented. "I have freedom to come and go as I please. My meals are eaten in the dining room where I enjoy the companionship of many good friends my age. If I don't feel well, my meals are brought to me. Maid service is provided for laundry and cleaning. There is always something to do—card games, musicals, crafts, movies. My children visit me frequently. I think I'm as happy as a man my age can expect to be. And best of all, I'm no burden to my children."

Fred, another elderly widower, is not financially able to live in the kind of residence Alex enjoys. After his wife died at the age of eighty, Fred remained in their small but comfortable home. His daughters live close by, and he never lacks invitations for dinner. He enjoys a community-sponsored meals-on-wheels program and a monthly visit from a public health nurse. Fred's church provides him with many social activities and he is an active member of the senior citizen club in his community. He says, "You don't have to be lonely if you just make the effort to keep involved with people. There are many opportunities for social support. You have to go after it!"

On the other hand, the young man whose wife dies is typically pressured to remarry whether or not he has children. Society believes every young man *naturally* should want a wife, particularly if he has been widowed. He needs sex; he should become a father if he is not one already. If he is a father, his children must have a mother. Don, for example, was a young man in his twenties, going places in the work world. He had a wife and three children, aged one month, two years, and four years, when his wife was killed in an automobile accident.

Don's situation was desperate. Typically, he could not find adequate care for his three babies. Fortunately, his mother could stay with them temporarily, and after a few months he was able to obtain live-in help for child care and household tasks.

As time passed, Don found there was much more to his desire to remarry than providing a mother for his children.

He explains, "One cannot be lonely with three babies in your home. But I missed having a woman in my home, someone to talk with, someone to sleep with, an adult with whom to share a loving, intimate relationship." Within a year after his wife died, he married a woman of twenty-two who had not been previously married.

Given the social pressures, along with their own personal needs, most young widowers do remarry. However, for the young widower who chooses to remain single, there is some support. The woman's liberation movement has encouraged people to resist the push toward marriage. Sex outside of marriage has become more acceptable and more readily available. Bachelorhood has even become glamorized. Men share apartments, which provides needed companionship and friendship. Ken, for example, a twenty-five-year-old widower, was severely criticized by his family because he decided not to remarry immediately. They were unhappy about his new life-style and wanted him to settle down into a stable relationship. He says, "My marriage was not all that blissful. My wife and I had many fights about spending money, and relationships with relatives and friends. Now I enjoy making decisions on my own instead of jointly. I like the flexibility of my daily schedule. I can spend money and go places spontaneously without any feeling of guilt. I enjoy the diversity of contacts with people. I enjoy the sexual freedom I have. Many possibilities are there. My wife was the only girl I went with, so if and when I do remarry, I will have a better idea of what kind of a woman is best for me."

Some widowers with children also remain unmarried. Steve, for example, had a ten-year-old daughter at home when his wife died. He says, "My daughter needs me, and I don't think she would adjust to my marrying again. She and I are very close; our relationship satisfies my need for love and companionship. We are real pals, and I am content with our family life just the way it is. My son is in college; he adds to my fulfillment. I am a man of financial means, so social life is no problem. I have joined some singles groups and have met other single men and women through my work. My sexual needs are met through a relationship with a divorced lady who also has no desire to remarry. She is a liberated professional woman married to a highly successful career."

Steve concludes, "I don't even feel single yet; I feel like a family man. My first marriage was very satisfying, and after five years, I still don't feel the need for another marriage. Maybe some day."

Perhaps Steve does not want to risk again the hurt he suffered when his wife died. Maybe he is waiting until his children are grown and on their own. Perhaps his needs are such that he will never emotionally get single again and, thus, will remain unmarried.

Other considerations also affect the widower's choice to remarry or to remain single. Doug, for example, says, "I am in poor financial straits, and within another year, I probably will be out of a job when my employer goes in for more automation. How can I take on a new wife—no matter how badly I might like to be married?" He has another reason for not remarrying—health: Doug is in the advanced stage of diabetes.

Al has had a heart condition for the past twenty years, and after his wife died, he felt he had no right ever to expect another woman to marry him. He asks, "Can I have happiness again? No, I can't expect another woman to sacrifice her life to care for a sick man."

Remaining single is one way of surviving after the death of one's wife. Remarriage is the alternative, and many factors enter into the decision. When a widower is twenty-seven, he will have different considerations than when he is sixty-five. A happy first marriage may turn him toward remarriage, while an unhappy first marriage may discourage him. If he is financially secure, he may prefer the mobility of not being married rather than tying himself down again. He may be motivated to remarry quickly "for the sake of the children," or he may decide to postpone marriage until the children have grown up and left home.

Will he remarry? That depends on the widower's expectations for his future. When a widower remarries, his expectations are as great as when he married the first time. Perhaps the expectations are more realistic, for he has learned about the requirements of a good marriage. He has made the mental adjustments necessary to marry again. He has hopes and expectations, and he looks forward to a beginning as well as to an end. This is the climax of his re-entry into the coupled world. Once again he and his wife will be one and accepted as such. No longer will he be a fifth wheel. No longer will well-meaning friends arrange chance dates. Once again his house will become a home. Once again there will be a feeling of warmth and love contained in those four walls. He knows there will be problems because he has been down the road before. The soon-to-remarry widower expects his mate to be someone who listens, who has an interest in his welfare, and who returns his love with honest feeling.

8

The Man Involuntarily
Separated From His Wife
by Long-Term Disability

THERE is a special population of newly single men who are neither divorced nor widowed, but separated from their wives following a physical or mental breakdown. In most cases the woman is institutionalized either permanently or for long periods at a time, unable to function in her usual role as wife, and where there were children, as mother.

These men have unique problems. While they experience many of the same emotions as divorced and widowed men, their "in limbo" status makes it difficult for them to get appropriate support. They face the special dilemma of being alone, yet are unable to mourn someone who is still living. Sometimes they have difficult medical decisions to make, adding to their burdens.

Information about these men is scarce. Few self-help groups are available for them, although many need professional help when support from family is inadequate.

The trauma of this kind of separation is often compounded by societal attitudes. As though their anguish and grief are not enough, their own integrity is sometimes questioned, similar to that of men whose wives commit suicide. Is he to blame? Could he have prevented what happened? The suspicious glances. The questions. The avoidance. The isolation from former friends, even accusations by family members.

Meeting needs for female companionship and sex is particularly difficult for these men. The guilt they feel even thinking about dating is far sharper than that felt by divorced or widowed men— their loyalty stands in the way. They cannot free themselves emotionally from a wife who is, but isn't. These circumstances postpone completion of the grief process for involuntarily separated men, and their special problems need to be revealed and understood.

The Separation

Clarence, a surgeon, was forty-four when his wife suffered a massive stroke ten years ago. Their children are Anne who was 18 months old, and Tim, who was four. Clarence's story is particularly poignant. He feels his pain even more acutely because he is a physician, and yet he could not help his own wife.

Clarence begins by saying, "Everything in my career, our marriage was on the upswing. I was packed to leave for an interview for a new and exciting position. I returned home from my office that tragic day and found the house empty. The phone rang. It was our neighbor, who said that I should hurry over—that while my wife, Claire, was visiting with her, she suddenly developed a terrible headache and was vomiting. I rushed over and brought Claire home. Then I took her in my car to the emergency hospital, where they examined her briefly before taking her to the intensive care unit. An hour or so later our doctor told me I should go to her and say my good-byes— that she would die shortly. I went to her, took her gently in my arms and we said good-bye, both of us believing she would die. Can you imagine having one hour to let go of a lifetime of being together?

"Our physician came into her room and murmured a few words and got out of there as quickly as he could. I felt a terrible numbness. I couldn't believe that she was dying. I wouldn't. We waited for death to come, hoping it wouldn't, and it didn't. She survived the stroke, and after waiting for a few days, it was decided that surgery might prevent further damage. The operation was a success. Her life was saved, but she was almost completely paralyzed. She had no movement in her limbs and could not speak. Five years later, however, through physical therapy she gained movement in her arms and hands, and her voice returned so that she was speaking clearly with good diction. Until her voice returned, she communicated with me by blinking her eyes and with a slight movement of her hands. No one would believe me at first that she was able to communicate in this way.

"The ambiguity of the situation was terrible—not knowing how long she would live, or if she would live went on for years. I don't think I denied what happened to her. I thought I was very realistic. It's hard to know what my feelings were. I took it where it was. I didn't know if she was going to recover, and she has not. The central feature of my life was being able to cope—to deal with whatever came my way. At this point in time, Claire has been institutionalized for ten years. She is completely bedridden. The extent of her mobility is the ability to move her arms.

"I did have to work through a lot of feelings, but anger wasn't one of them, at least at first," Clarence continues. "I had some real guilt feelings. I knew what to do about strokes, and I feel that I should not have taken her home first before taking her to the hospital. I did seek therapy for myself and was helped in coping with guilt feelings. I know now that I did what I thought was best—I just did not believe that my wife was really having a stroke.

"I wasn't angry at God, as I've heard many men are in such circumstances. As my therapist said, 'You are an atheist, you don't even have a God to be angry at!' I know that I was lonely. I missed the companionship of an adult woman very much. And as I said, my situation has been so ambiguous. There is no finality. I haven't had the orgasm of grief from knowing that life with my wife is ended so that I can go on in a normal way.

"In the first months I often had periods of depression. I felt, 'What's the use of it all? Why me?' I sometime lost my appetite. Had sleepless nights. I lived in the country, and I felt isolated. I used to feel that my life was completely shattered. Another thing, my wife's illness occurred in October during the time of my birthday, our daughter's birthday, and right before Thanksgiving and Christmas— the worst possible time of the year. It was a very sad period for us, and this was also at the time when my work becomes the busiest, so the stress I faced was almost unbearable at times. This early period after her illness was absolutely devastating for me.

"I felt such pain for my Claire. My only thoughts were of what I could do to make her life more bearable. During the early part of her hospitalization in the nursing home I used to help her sexually. I would masturbate her to orgasm. But the damnable nursing home was so miserably against what I was doing, that after some really searing experiences I eventually was forced to give up, and I have not given her any help with her sexual needs for a long while. They wouldn't give us any privacy once they discovered our sexual activities. They even went so far as to insist that her door be kept open during my visits. Along with all the tremendous pressures I felt with my work and raising the children alone, I just couldn't fight it. I just didn't have the energy to fight the system.

"My wife has been practically a 'vegetable' relative to having a normal life. I believe loyalty to your partner is important, and it is important also to respond to each other's needs. To engage in mutually rewarding kinds of things. My wife loves me, and I have tried to give her love in return. That may be a rationalization, but it is why I have been loyal to my wife and remained celibate for several years."

Coping With Grief

The ways Clarence copes with his feelings of guilt, helplessness, sadness, and hopelessness are similar to those used by men whose wives have died. He submerges himself in his work. He consults a therapist. He has support from his family. But typically, his friends do not seem to be able to help. He says, "My friends couldn't handle talking about my wife. I might cry, and they wouldn't like that. After my wife's illness I didn't get any invitations from the couples we used to socialize with. They couldn't handle the fact that I might talk about her. That was too real, and they didn't want to have to face this reality. I also felt some of our friends blamed me for what happened to Claire. I have had to make new friends. I have not made social friendships at the hospital, and no one there talks to me about my wife."

As in the case of divorced and widowed men, men whose wives are institutionalized find that they, too, are deserted by former friends. Norm, a sixty-five-year-old widower, feels that perhaps his married friends avoid him because they are too uncomfortable with the possibility of seeing him cry. Craig, a thirty-five-year-old divorced physician, faces the same problem as Clarence. None of his colleagues give him emotional support. If they say anything at all, it is some comment about his being on the prowl for eager females.

Michael, a forty-six-year-old professor whose wife has been in a mental institution for the past five years cannot understand why he was dropped from the social lists of his married friends. He says, "I was hurt by the seeming lack of concern from fellow professors at the university, but being ignored by so many of our married friends really hurt. They acted as though I was somehow to blame for my wife's mental condition. How else can I explain their hesitancy to include me in their social life?" The "fifth-wheel syndrome"—being left out of the coupled world—is experienced by most formerly married people, and the man whose wife is institutionalized for mental or physical reasons is no exception. It is painful, and particularly so for men who have so few outlets for their feelings.

Clarence believes it is cruel that society views men as having no problems they cannot easily deal with. He says, "Men have many inhibitions that prevent them from reaching for help—for someone to talk with—and yet friends seldom offer a shoulder upon which to cry. Women need men to be strong. They don't expect us to cry. As mothers, they condition their sons to be strong, manly, not to cry when hurt.

"Fortunately, I have been able to cry. My mother, mother-in-law, and sister listened to me as I talked about my feelings and have been extremely supportive." Clarence suggests that a man in his situation find a family member or close friend with whom he can open his heart and share his grief. "It is hard to talk about personal feelings. The only one I could bare my soul to was my wife, and I can't burden her since her stroke. She would not be up to that," he says.

"When my wife became ill, I felt people expected to believe that I was managing okay. That as a man, I could handle any situation with little outside help. The standard way in which people greeted me was to ask me how Claire was, and sometimes I would walk away without telling them, because talking was painful. And they would ask me how the children were, but they never asked how I was. I suppose it is in many ways more upsetting to people to see a man cry than to see a woman cry. I know that in counseling medical students I am more surprised to see a man break down than a woman, but now I have learned to empathize with both men and women.

"Groups help some people cope with their grief. There are organizations such as Parents Without Partners but I've never felt comfortable there. I am neither widowed nor divorced. I don't fit. I felt very uncomfortable in a situation where I was subjected to the dating game, because until very recently I had not felt I was in the position to date. Support groups were not for me."

Clarence feels very alone. Typically, his wife was his only confidante. When a man loses his confidante, he really has no one else to turn to, because men rarely exchange intimate details of their lives with each other. For this reason, female companionship becomes imperative for the man alone. He wants a woman who will lend a sympathetic ear. If he has children to care for, he is fortunate because they can keep him from "wallowing in his own grief," as one widower remarks. But children, of course, are unable to fill all of a lonely man's emotional needs.

The Separated Man as Single Parent

Clarence also has a special problem with his children. "Both of them are adopted, and one of the best-kept secrets about adoption is the emotional trauma a child suffers from being separated from its natural mother," he says. "Both of our children had been torn away from the fundamental safety of a trustworthy relationship. This trust had been destroyed, and we were in the process of rebuilding it when Claire became ill. This was probably more of a problem for Tim because we had just about re-established a trusting relationship with him. Anne was halfway into adjusting to a new trust, so her mother's illness has not affected her as much as it has Tim. This is not to say she was unaffected. She has developed into a very strong-minded little girl who can hold her own."

Clarence believes that how well a man copes depends a lot upon whether he has children. He had momentary feelings of helplessness in the early stages of his wife's illness, but it was not a central theme for him. He was an accomplished cook and always did a good share of child care. He knew how to run the house, although after his wife was gone, having the entire responsibility was draining at times.

"I feel fortunate that my children have kept me from feeling alone," he said. "In fact, I think the most important thing about my children is that they really kept me involved with life. I would have been far worse off if I hadn't had them. They saved me from the temptation to crawl off in a corner and withdraw. I have known a number of widowers in their seventies who just didn't live very long after they lost their wives. They had little incentive to live, being so alone.

"Perhaps I all too often succumbed to the temptation of seeing that my children were cared for at the expense of my own life, in a way that went beyond reason. I could have fought harder to find others to care for my children and free myself to become more social in the early days of my wife's absence. It was difficult. I lost out on a lot of living. I should not have tried to provide such perfect care for my children all the time. Probably guilt caused me to overcompensate for the loss of their mother."

Clarence says single women find more support in getting help with their children, such as by exchanging baby-sitting. "I never found a single male parent I could exchange baby sitting with," he recalls. "And I couldn't do this sort of thing with a single mother unless it involved some kind of social relationship, and I did not want that. I felt uncomfortable in a situation where a woman expected some kind of social attachment when I was not ready.

"My concern was over my children's welfare, and my emotions were involved with my wife's tragic illness. Losing their mother was a terrible burden on my children. Now they fear that something might happen to me. Resolving this normal fear is one of the most important things a man responsible for his children's care and welfare must attend to. In retrospect, our children have developed very well both emotionally and physically. We manage quite well as a family."

Clarence faces many of the same problems widowers face as single fathers. He feels particularly emphatic that having children is a positive force in his life. They keep him from being unbearably lonely and force him into activities that take his mind off his own despair.

Return to Normalcy: Dating

Insofar as relationships with other women are concerned, Clarence says, "I think the best way a person can honor the spirit and memory of someone else is to get back into life as quickly as possible. Before she became ill, what my wife gave me was a reinforcement of my love of life. To deny my love of life would be to deny her. I tend to think, to see, and to be very much in touch with the tragedies of life.

Heaven knows, as a physician I have many opportunities to witness tragedies. I have an image of making a feast among the ashes. We all have ashes, and the trick is to make the feast anyway. Not to deny the ashes, but not to be worn down by them. It is difficult to live with tragedy. I think it is important to celebrate life—to find ways to express one's feelings."

Clarence points out that his is a special situation—he has and yet has not lost his wife. Although it seems important to him to go through the grieving process before looking for a new relationship, it has been difficult because there is no finality to his relationship with his wife. "It's so easy to wait for others to reach out to you, but the fact is that the world is not going to reach out to you," he says. "I've gone through the whole range of things, feeling sorry for myself, wondering why me? Then I realized that it is necessary to grieve and then get back to living. I realized I had to find my own companionship, but if there are going to be friendships, I had to be ready."

Clarence says men in his situation must expect that the first time they go out alone, they may have problems. "You go to a party and you may feel alone—but you have to go out so that people can find you and reach out to you as you reach out to them. If you say it's going to be all right, it will be all right." He chooses events that offer potential for meeting interesting people, both men and women. He avoids bars and thinks people who go to them to find companionship are usually disappointed.

"I have been fortunate to live in a large city near a university campus where I find many opportunities to meet interesting people," he said. "There are a variety of singles clubs in my city, although you have to be selective because some of them are just, frankly, very opportunistic. I was fortunate to get in touch with a group of people who were single when I was a 'little out of water,' and I made sure when I was with this group that everyone knew I was not really single since my wife is still living. I didn't want to fly under false colors. This group had a variety of people with varying interests. It was not deeply satisfying, but it certainly beat sitting around home feeling sorry for myself. This was a caring group, a companionable group.

"When I first began to think I wanted to date, I had painful, conflicting thoughts because at that time I was not committed to the idea that my wife might not get well, although we knew she wouldn't," he says. "I found I had a lot of guilt feelings about wanting to date."

Fortunately, Clarence's first date was initiated by a woman at work, and other women his age have indicated an interest in dating him. He suspects some of these women are interested in him because he is safe—he can't get married because his wife is still alive. Several times a relationship went sour because of the possibility that Clarence might not be so safe—he might divorce his wife.

"I have resolved my guilt about dating, for a man should be able to have some companionship and love with a woman, and I can't have that with my wife," he says. Clarence is selective about the women he dates, usually choosing someone productive and engaged in the world around her. "It is good to date a variety of women, because I can say I have learned and gotten something from every relationship that I have had, and from every woman I have known well," he says.

Thoughts of Remarriage

Clarence believes we are all ambivalent about intimacy, having both positive and negative feelings. He thinks that in general, in relationships there is a coming together and then a necessary separation, and he sometimes thinks it would be too much for him to contemplate the total commitment of marriage. Yet after ten years of separation from his wife, Clarence became involved in a relationship he hopes will become permanent. For the past year he has been dating a woman he met in the nursing home where his wife is a patient, and they have developed a love for each other that makes them want to live together. Betty does not want him to divorce Claire for fear of the hurt it might cause Claire. Betty understands Clarence still loves his wife in a caring way, but his love has not grown or developed since her stroke—it's a historical love.

"Betty and I would be content to live together without marriage," he says, "but we are concerned about how the children would take this. Teenagers go for the jugular! Betty has two children by her previous marriage who are about the same age as mine. She is a lovely woman, and my children love her, but we have not spoken to them about marriage. I really want this. I feel that my son Tim at age fifteen is rather indifferent, but Anne, now twelve, is more inclined to resent my relationship with Betty. Anne and I have a close relationship, and she isn't willing to share that. It was okay with Anne that Betty lived with us this summer, but there were times when she seemed jealous. She wants our house to be ours, and she resents it when I include Betty in any discussion about the house—redecorating or anything else. Well, a family has an existence, and if we then put two families together, original families go out of existence in a philosophical sense, and my daughter has had enough break-ups in her life. She is especially afraid that the family which is so important to her will cease to be."

Clarence sometimes thinks it must be possible to put something together that others wouldn't call a family—a group that perhaps lives together and gets along. Betty and he are very much aware of the difficulties they will have joining two families. "But this does not make sense to me. I have sacrificed a great deal—ten years—to my children and it does not make sense now to give up the opportunity I have for happiness with Betty. I can't cater to my children forever." He has not raised the issue of marriage with Anne because Betty and he have not made the decision yet. It is a remote possibility right now—at least another year.

"My wife is certainly unaware," Clarence said. "She has been institutionalized for ten years and doesn't know anything about the world around her. Her only interest is wanting to know a little about the children, although they seldom go to see her now. Tim hasn't been to see her for two or three years, and Anne usually can find some reason why she can't go to see her mother. And I am very sympathetic about this. She was just an infant when her mother became ill, and there is not much of a tie between them. I have given them a hard time about not seeing their mother at first, and it might have been much better had I never pushed their visits. But I was thinking of my wife's needs.

"I do get angry at my situation. It may be that I am angry and frustrated because I have felt so helpless in remedying many of my problems. It's very hard to find out whom to be angry at."

Clarence says his situation has slowly improved. Betty and he do not live together, but they see each other often, as often as their two busy careers will allow. When they did live together this summer while her teenage son was away, it was wonderful, and he now misses her daily presence in his home. "I think we felt freer both to be together and to be apart," he says. "Now that we are physically separated, we miss the freedom to make plans to do things together. Things are more stilted. The dailiness is really the deep part of what marriage is about.

"I now feel free to divorce my wife so that I can have a marriage on a straight emotional basis. But it would be extremely complex financially and legally. I went along for a number of years knowing that I couldn't divorce my wife. Now the laws have changed, but financially the situation is very difficult. However, I am prepared to go through with the divorce as soon as we decide that we want to get married. That is a decision we are considering now."

Clarence says he has felt typical societal pressure to remarry. "My family is very happy about my relationship with Betty. They have been aware of the kind of pain my wife's condition has caused me. Even my wife's mother is very supportive of my relationship with Betty. I knew my mother-in-law was a big person, but I didn't know if she could be that big.

"The way I told her was to assure her that I would always continue to care about my wife—her daughter—and that I didn't have plans to stop seeing Claire should I divorce and remarry. I would continue to care about her, and I really do. Whenever I go to see her, there is lots of warmth between us, and there is no reason that our loving relationship should end with my remarrying. And it wouldn't take anything away from my new relationship. Betty is very supportive of the feelings I have for my wife, and she said she would be very unhappy if I stopped seeing Claire. Betty's compassion is very rare—I have had relationships where the lady was not tolerant of my situation. If I spent a lot of time with Claire, that would be a different story, but the little time I do spend with her does not take away from any other relationships I may have."

Clarence believes there are all kinds of love: love of a parent for a child, love among friends, and passionate love that involves sex between lovers. He views his love for his wife as historic. It has not grown since her illness, and it is not really related to today as much as to yesterday. "The aspect of love which might induce jealousy is just not there," he says. "It is just a matter of caring for someone. Not just feeling responsible for her, but really feeling very warmly toward her. I will have this warm feeling for Claire as long as I live. It is important that the woman I now love understands my feelings for my wife. I couldn't cope with anything else.

"My thoughts are now that within the next year Betty and I will marry, and recently I received some wonderful encouragement—my son told me he thought it was about time that I divorced his mother so that I could live a normal, happily married life with Betty."

Just as many widowers and divorced men hold positive views toward remarriage, Clarence has come to terms with his emotions and feels ready to marry again. His dilemma is compounded by the fact that although his marital relationship ended with his wife's stroke, he has not experienced the finality that death gives to a relationship. However, his needs for intimacy, love, sex, and daily togetherness have become paramount, and we can hope that any remaining barriers to marriage will be soon removed. Clarence deserves a happy, satisfying marriage.

9

How to Help the Single-Again Man

T HE stresses that accompany a serious loss are extreme for everyone concerned, and many newly single men feel that support services to help them cope with loss and adjust to a new life are sadly lacking.

A widower suffers grief not only immediately following the death of his wife but often for years afterward. A divorced man most likely endures emotional pain during the decision-making process, at the time of separation, and often for months and years after the divorce is final. The man whose wife is separated from him because of mental or physical incapacitation begins grief when his wife becomes incapacitated and is institutionalized, but he cannot complete his mourning. He has and he has not lost a wife.

Divorced Men

Divorce is a complex matter that may be explained in stages. Paul Bohannan, a social scientist, uses six phases to explain the divorce process. In each phase, support from family, friends, and professionals may be useful. The first phase is the emotional divorce, which centers around the desire to end an unsatisfactory marriage. Before the second phase, or legal divorce, the marriage may have ended emotionally for one or both of the marriage partners. Divorce mediation in this second phase is often helpful for couples with cooperative attitudes to reach mutual decisions, such as division of assets and child custody. Family support also can be helpful during this phase by providing comfort and opportunity to vent feelings.

The third phase is the economic divorce. This phase is one of the more difficult. Anger, guilt, and hostility often interfere with necessary compromises, particularly when a wife has a substantial income of her own. A divorce counselor is helpful in making equitable property settlements and child custody decisions.

The fourth phase, according to Bohannan, is the co-parental divorce, which deals with custody, child support, and visitation. While most divorced fathers report that they are "part-time" fathers, they are satisfied that their relationship with their children remains strong.

The fifth phase is the public divorce. It is often difficult to announce to a couple's community—relatives, friends, work colleagues—that one has been divorced. As Bohannan suggests, this announcement is often delayed because of the fear of negative reactions. During this difficult phase, loving support is most important to counter possible negative reactions from relatives, friends, and work colleagues.

The final phase is the psychic divorce, in which the person must deal with the development of a single life-style. Men who have the least difficulty in establishing a new social network and adjusting to living without a spouse include those with higher educational attainment and socio-economic resources; those who are aware of the availability of counseling services and who utilize professional help when necessary; and those who receive strong emotional support from family and friends. The length of time taken to accept their single-again style varies. However, older men generally have a more difficult time adjusting than younger men because there are fewer people in their age category to whom to relate, and they have become accustomed to married life over the years.

The suggestion to seek help from a counselor or psychotherapist sometimes meets with a negative reaction, varying from expressions of embarrassment, fear of expressing one's private self to others, lack of time, and even an antagonistic attitude toward clinicians. There is still a stigma attached to men who seek help from professional counselors. Doesn't a "real" man handle his problems by himself?

When a man is in a crisis and unable to handle his emotions, he needs encouragement to let go of his feelings. The formerly married man's loneliness is aggravated by the traditional male sex role, which keeps him from revealing his pain. Many divorced men have feelings of low self-esteem. They miss their home and former life styles. They are lonely men. Their anger, guilt, resentment, and sadness may be more than they can handle by themselves.

A man must put aside the pretense, the denial that he is in pain. He must accept the emotional pain and realize that it will take a while before he is completely well again, that no one is entirely to blame for what has happened. He needs to know it is okay to feel depressed; that it is okay to feel anger toward his former wife, God, or society, and he should be provided a means to vent these negative feelings. He should be encouraged to do nice things for himself; to pamper himself with a trip out of town, see a good play, entertain some good friends. As he begins to heal, he needs to know it's okay not to feel depressed or sad, or lonely. His thoughts of his situation, as well as his behavior, will become more positive as he is gently assisted through the healing process. His sense of self esteem will grow and his anger and resentment will subside.

Widowers

Four stages of bereavement can be pinpointed, each stage requiring different kinds of therapeutic support. In the first stage, awaiting the imminent death of a loved one, emotional stress is high and unyielding. An invitation to dinner or a movie may be more valuable than any kind of therapy at this point. A man needs help to handle feelings of guilt and unresolved, distressing aspects of the relationship with his wife. He should be encouraged to take on responsibilities that only he can handle but to turn over lesser tasks to others, to recognize and accept his limitations at this time, and to begin thinking about what life will be like after the death occurs.

At the time of death—the second stage—feelings are likely to be overwhelming, and depression will be constant. For the widower whose wife died suddenly and unexpectedly, the second stage may involve extreme shock and disbelief. He needs the opportunity to discuss the past and present and to look to the future. It is important for him to explore what the loss means in the present, and to be allowed to grieve openly.

During the third stage, the weeks following the death, grief remains severe. This is a time for the expression of feelings, especially for men who keep their feelings inside.

Some widowers may continue for years without completing their grief process, and help may be needed to get them through this fourth stage of bereavement, to "let go" of the dead person.

During the early stages of bereavement, when grief is at its worst, some men need medication. Some need group activities to adjust to being alone. Relatives and friends can be helpful if they accept the widower's need to grieve, express their empathy, and provide support.

Widowers are often helped by a person who will let them ventilate their feelings, encourage them to face reality, deal with the present and future rather than the past, and recognize that their guilt, anger, and depression are common, normal reactions.

Some men have long-standing, complex problems that go beyond strategies of ventilation, support, understanding, and acceptance. They may need to seek specialized help.

The Involuntarily Separated

Probably the greatest assistance for a man whose wife is institution-alized is to see him through his grief and help him "let go" of his marital relationship. Living is very difficult for a man who has but does not have a wife.

It is the loss of a caring relationship that is most grievous for these men—someone to talk with, to sleep with, to share tasks with. Eventually they understand that a new, caring relationship might be the answer.

Coping involves not only dealing with immediate stress but also making sense of it. The inability to achieve and maintain a sense that things will work out may seriously hinder the balance necessary for emotional health.

Specific Problems

Health

Coping with grief and depression are the primary problems of the single-again man, but he should also be aware that emotional stress is likely to manifest itself in physical problems. Although he may resist, he should be encouraged to have a thorough physical exam. He needs to exercise and eat properly. Often because of despair, loneliness, or lack of knowledge, single-again men neglect their nutritional needs.

Dependency on alcohol is common among grieving men and women. It is an unhealthy habit. It is far better for the single-again man to learn about good nutrition and exercise and to adopt a healthy regimen.

Financial Problems

Statistics indicate that widowed men ages sixty to seventy-nine are much poorer than their married counterparts, and most live alone. Children are less likely to provide economic and emotional support for widowers than for widows. Older divorced or separated men, like widowers, are much poorer than their married counterparts. They are the poorest of single-again men, and most live alone. Their isolation from children is much greater than for older divorced or separated women, and women receive more social support than men from family and friends.

Men from lower socioeconomic backgrounds tend to have the most difficulty coping. These men usually are not seen by counselors for two reasons: lack of money and lack of knowledge about availability of or need for counseling.

The U.S. Bureau of Census reported in 1985 that approximately 46 percent of widowers in the United States were living at or near the poverty level, with an annual income ranging from $1,000 to $9,999. Divorced men are younger as a group than widowers, yet 25 percent are living at or near the poverty level.

Sources of Help

For group support, try Parents Without Partners, an international, not-for-profit, nonsectarian educational organization devoted to the welfare and interests of single parents and their children. Many singles' groups are sponsored locally by church and community organizations. A phone call to a church office, local YMCA or YWCA, Young Men's Health Association or Young Women's Health Association, or a family counseling clinic may provide information about the community services and organizations that are available.

Groups and programs specifically for widowed persons have been established on both the local and national levels. NAIM is a national organization sponsored by the Catholic Church to serve the spiritual and emotional needs of widowed men and women. The story is that a widow in this village NAIM had a son who died and the Lord restored him to life to provide some happiness for the widow. Referrals for grief counseling may be obtained through one's religious affiliation, mental health association, or public health department.

Although at this time services specifically for newly single men are minimal, those who reach out for help can find it if they persevere. Single-again men need and deserve support. Groups at the national level which may provide help for single-again men include:

American Divorce Association for Men 9318
1008 White Oak
Arlington Heights, IL 60005

America's Society of Separated & Divorced Men 9319
575 Keep St.
Elgin, IL 60120

Free Men 12726
212 Tenth St., S.E.
Washington, D.C. 2003

Men's Resource Center 9607
3534 S.E. Main
Portland, OR 97214

Men's Rights' Association 12729
P.O. Box 189
Forest Lake, MN 55025

National Congress for Men 12730
P.O. Box 147
Mendham, NJ 07945

National Association for Widowed Persons 10136
P.O. Box 3564
Springfield, IL 62708

Many men say they receive their most significant immediate support from close family members and friends. If you want to help, offer to do household tasks and prepare meals. Offer child care.

It is important for family and friends to realize how painful social isolation is for the newly single man. Because loneliness is a major problem for newly single men, it is helpful to let him know he is welcome in your home not only for Sunday night family suppers but also for those Saturday night parties.

Friends and family can be very helpful to single-again men who may be in need of various kinds of support—emotional, social, physical, and economic. Hopefully this book will encourage support for the single-again man. It is a harmful myth that men can handle any and all problems without any help.

Selected Readings

Chapter 1

S. L. Albrecht, "Reactions and Adjustments to Divorce: Differences in the Experiences of Males and Females," *Family Relations* 29, (1980), 59–68.

R. O. Blood and M. C. Blood, "Amicable Divorce," *Alternative Lifestyles* 2 (1979), 4:483–498.

B. L. Bloom, *Changing Patterns of Psychiatric Care* (New York: Human Sciences, 1975).

_____S. J. Asher, and S. W. White, "Marital Disruption as a Distressor: A Review and Analysis," *Psychological Bulletin* 84, (July, 1978), 867–894.

_____W. F. Hodges, R. A. Caldwell, L. Systra, and A. R. Cedrone, "Marital Separation: A Community Survey," *Journal of Divorce* 3, (Fall, 1979), 7–19.

_____W. Hodges, and R. Caldwell, "Marital Separation: The First Eight Months," in E. Callahan & K. McCluskey, eds., *Life-Span Developmental Psychology* (New York: Academic Press, 1983), 217–239.

P. Bohannan, "The Six Stations of Divorce," in P. Bohannan, ed., *Divorce and After* (Garden City, N.Y.: Doubleday, 1979), 33–62.

Jean Brody, *Divorce-Case Studies* (New York: Simon and Schuster, 1980).

P. Brown, B. Felton, V. Whiteman & R. Manela, "Attachment and Distress Following Marital Separation," *Journal of Divorce* 3 (1980), 303–317.

Cheryl Buehler, "Initiator Status and Divorce Transition," Paper presented at the National Council on Family Relations Annual Meeting (Detroit, 1986).

Jane Burgess & W. Kohn, *The Widower* (Boston: Beacon Press, 1978).

D. A. Chiriboga, "Marital Separation and Stress." *Alternative Lifestyles* 2 (November, 1979), 461–470.

_____and L. Cutler, "Stress Responses Among Divorcing Men and Women," *Journal of Divorce* 1 (Winter, 1977), 95–106.

_____J. Roberts and J. A. Stein, "Psychological Well-Being During Marital Separation," *Journal of Divorce* 2 (Fall, 1978), 21–36.

James L. Framo, "The Friendly Divorce," *Psychology Today* 11 (February, 1978), 77–80, 99–102.

W. Goode, *After Divorce* (New York: The Free Press, 1956).

Earl A. Grollman, *Concerning Death: A Practical Guide for the Living* (Boston: Beacon Press, 1974).

Herbert Hyman, *Of Time and Widowhood* (Durham, N.C.: Duke University Press, 1983).

M. Kolevzon & S. Gottlieb, "The Impact of Divorce: A Multivariate Study," *Journal of Divorce* 7 (1983), 89–98.

Elisabeth Kübler-Ross, *On Death and Dying* (New York: The Macmillan Co., Inc., 1969).

_____*Death: The Final Stage of Growth* (Englewood Cliffs, N.J.: Prentice Hall, Inc., 1975).

C. M. Parkes, "The Effects of Bereavement on Physical and Mental Health—A Study of the Medical Records of Widows," *British Medical Journal* 2 (1964), 274–279.

_____*Bereavement* (New York: International Universities Press, 1972).

_____"Determinants of Outcome Following Bereavement," *Omega* 6 (1975).

E. Pettit & B. Bloom, "Whose Decision Was It? The Effects of Initiator Status on Adjustment to Marital Disruption," *Journal of Marriage and the Family* 46 (1984), 587–595.

Elin Schoen & Pat Golbitz, *Widower* (Morrow, 1984).

Robert S. Weiss, "The Emotional Impact of Marital Separation," *Single Life*, ed. Peter J. Stein (New York: St. Martin's Press, 1981), 69–77.

R. S. Weiss, *Loneliness* (Cambridge, Mass.: MIT Press, 1973.

_____*Marital Separation* (New York: Basic Books, 1975).

Chapter 2

C. Brisco and J. B. Smith, "Depression and Marital Turmoil," *Archives of General Psychiatry* 29 (December, 1973), 811–817.

_____E. Robins, S. Martin, and F. Gaskin, "Divorce and Psychiatric Disease," *Archives of General Psychiatry* 29 (July, 1973), 119–125.

B. B. Brown, "Who Shall I Turn To? Social and Psychological Determinants of Helpseeking Among Urban Adults," *American Journal of Community Psychology* 6 (October, 1978), 425–439.

Elizabeth Cauhape, *Fresh Starts: Men & Women After Divorce* (New York: Basic Books, 1983).

P. J. Clayton, J. A. Halikas, & W. L. Maurice, "The Depression of Widowhood," *British Journal of Psychiatry* 120 (1972), 71–77.

Bruce Fisher, *Rebuilding When Your Relationship Ends* (San Luis Obispo, Calif.: Impact, 1981).

S. J. Herrman, "Divorce: A Grief Process," *Perspectives in Psychiatric Care* (Spring, 1974), 108–112.

M. Hunt and B. Hunt, *The Divorce Experience* (New York: McGraw-Hill, 1977).

Leonard Kerpelman, *Divorce: A Guide For Men* (Icarus, 1983).

Mel Krantzler, *Creative Divorce* (New York: Signet, 1973).

Adele Rice Nudel, *Starting Over: Help for Young Widows and Widowers* (New York: Dodd, Mead, 1986).

C. M. Parkes, B. Benjamin & R. G. Fitzgerald, "Broken Heart: A Statistical Study of Increased Mortality Among Widowers,: *British Medical Journal* 1 (1969), 740–743.

_____& R. Brown, "Health After Bereavement: A Controlled Study of Young Boston Widows and Widowers," *Psychosomatic Medicine* 34 (1972), 449–461.

_____& R. S. Weiss, *Recovery from Bereavement* (New York: Basic Books, 1972).

B. Raphael, *The Anatomy of Bereavement* (New York: Basic Books, 1983).

G. Spanier & L. Thompson, "Relief and Distress after Marital Separation," *Journal of Divorce* 7 (1983), 31–49.

_____& L. Thompson, *Parting: The Aftermath of Separation and Divorce* (Beverly Hills: Sage, 1984).

R. W. Weiss, *Marital Separation* (New York: Basic Books, 1975).

J. W. Worden, *Grief Counseling and Grief Therapy* (New York: Springer, 1982).

M. Young, B. Benjamin & C. Wallis, "The Mortality of Widowers," *Lancet* 2 (1982), 454–456.

A. Zeiss, R. Zeiss & S. Johnson, "Sex Differences in Initiation of and Adjustment of Divorce," *Journal of Divorce* 4 (1980), 21–33.

Chapter 3

Mary Jo Bane, "Marital Disruption and the Lives of Children," *Journal of Social Issues* 32 (1976), 103–17.

J. Bowlby, "Childhood Mourning and its Implications for Psychiatry," *American Journal of Psychiatry* 118 (1961), 481–498.

Avis Brenner, *Helping Children Cope with Stress* (Lexington, Mass.: Lexington Books, 1984).

G. Brown, "Early Loss and Depression," in C. M. Parkes & J. Stevenson-Hinde, eds., *The Place of Attachment in Human Behavior* (New York: Basic Books, 1982).

Larry L. Bumpass and Ronald R. Rindfuss, "Children's Experience of Marital Disruption," *American Journal of Sociology* 85 (1979), 49–65.

Judith Cassetty, *The Parental Child-Support Obligation: Research, Practice, and Social Policy* (Lexington, Mass.: Lexington Books, 1983).

Elizabeth Dahl, "Parental Divorce and the Young Adult," *Family Strengths No. 5 Continuity and Diversity* edited by George Rowe, John DeFrain, Nick Stinett, Sally VanZandt (Newton: Mass.: Education Development Center, Inc., 1984), 209–223.

Esther Devall, Zolinda Stoneman, and Gene Brady, "The Impact of Divorce and Maternal Employment on Pre-Adolescent Children," *Journal of Family Relations* Vol. 35, No. 1 (January, 1986), 153–176.

S. A. Dramond, *Helping Children of Divorce: A Handbook for Parents and Teachers* (New York: Schocken Books, 1985).

R. D. Felner, M. A. Ginter, M. F. Boike & E. L. Cowan, "Parental Death or Divorce and the School Adjustment of Young Children," *American Journal of Community Psychology* 9 (1981), 181–191.

G. L. Fox, "Daughters of Divorce: The Roles of Fathers and Father-Figures in the Lives of Adolescent Girls Following Divorce," Unpublished Manuscript (1981).

F. F. Furstenberg, Jr., C. W. Nord, J. L. Peterson, and N. Zill, "A Life Course of Children of Divorce: Marital Disruption and Parental Contact," Paper presented at the Annual Meeting of Population Association of America, San Diego, Calif. (April 1982).

Earl Grollman, ed., *Explaining Death to Children* (Boston: Beacon Press, 1967).

_____*Talking About Death* (Boston: Beacon Press, 1976).

S. M. Grossman, J. A. Shea, & G. R. Adams, "Effects of Parental Divorce During Early Childhood on Ego Development and Identity Formation of College Students," *Journal of Divorce* 3 (1980), 263–270.

John Guidubaldi, Helen K. Cleminshaw, Joseph D. Perry, Bonnie K. Nastasi, and Jeanine Lightel, "The Role of Selected Family Environment Factors in Children's Post Divorce Adjustment," *Journal of Family Relations* Vol. 35, No. 1 (January, 1986), 141–151.

R. J. Kastenbaum, "The Child's Understanding of Death: How Does It Develop? In E. A. Grollman ed., *Explaining Death To Children* (Boston: Beacon Press, 1976).

Julia Lewis, "Children of Divorce: Long Term Outcome," *Medical Aspects of Human Sexuality* Vol. 19, No. 4 (April, 1985), 132–139.

Deborah Anna Luepnitz, *Child Custody: A Study of Families After Divorce* (Lexington, Mass.: Lexington Books, 1982).

Daniel P. Mueller and Philip W. Cooper, "Children of Single Parent Families: How They Fare as Young Adults," *The Journal of Family Relations* Vol. 35, No. 1 (January, 1986), 169–181.

Therese A. Rando, *Loss and Anticipatory Grief* (Lexington, Mass.: Lexington Books, 1986).

H. J. Rashke and K. D. Barringer, "Postdivorce Adjustment Among Persons Participating in Parents-Without-Partners Organizations," *Family Perspective* 11, (Winter), 23–34.

Helen Rosen, "Coping with Childhood Sibling Loss," *Unspoken Grief* (Lexington, Mass.: Lexington Books, 1985).

M. Rutter, "Parent-Child Separation: Psychological Effects on the Children," *Journal of Child Psychology and Psychiatry* 12 (1979), 233–260.

Judith Wallerstein and Joan Kelly, "The Effects of Parental Divorce: The Adolescent Experience," In J. Anthony and C. Koupernik, ed., *The Child in His Family: Children at Psychiatric Risk* (New York: Wiley, 1974).

_____"The Effects of Parental Divorce: Experiences of the Preschool Child," *Journal of the American Academy of Child Psychiatry* 14 (1975).

_____"The Effects of Parental Divorce: Experiences of the Child in Later Latency," *American Journal of Orthopsychiatry* 46 (April, 1976), 257–269.

_____*Surviving the Break-up: How Children Actually Cope with Divorce* (New York: Basic Books, 1980).

Chapter 4

A. Abarbanel, "Shared Parenting After Separation and Divorce: A Study of Joint Custody," *American Journal of Orthopsychiatry* 49(2) (1979), 320–329.

C. R. Ahrons, "Joint Custody Agreements in the Postdivorce Family," *Journal of Divorce* 3(3) (1980), 189–205.

Henry B. Biller, *Father, Child and Sex Roles* (Lexington, Mass: D.C. Heath and Co., 1971).

J. K. Burgess, "The Single Parent Family: A Social and Sociological Problem," *The Family Coordinator* 19 (1969), 137–144.

_____and W. Kohn, *The Widower* (Boston: Beacon Press, 1978).

A. Cherlin, J. Griffith and J. McCarthy, "A Note on Maritally Disrupted Men's Reports of Child Support in the June 1980 Current Population Survey," *Demography* 20(3) (1983), 385–390.

J. Defrain and R. Eirick, "Coping as Divorced Parents. A Comparative Study of Fathers and Mothers," *Family Relations* 30 (1981), 265–274.

L. Greer Fox, "Noncustodial Father," *Dimensions of Fatherhood* ed., Shirley M. Hanson and F. W. Bozett (Beverly Hills: Sage Publications, 1985), 293–413.

J. B. Greif, "Fathers, Children, and Joint Custody," *American Journal of Orthopsychiatry*, 49 (1979), 311–319.

_____*Single Fathers* (Lexington, Mass.: Lexington Books, 1985).

Marshall Hamilton, *Fathers' Influence on Children*, (Chicago: Nelson Hall, 1977).

Shirley Hanson, "Single Custodial Fathers," *Dimensions of Fatherhood* ed., Shirley M. Hanson and F. W. Bozett (Beverly Hills: Sage Publications, 1985), 369–392.

_____and Michael J. Sporakowski, "Single Parent Families," *Family Relations*, Vol. 35, No. 1, (January, 1986), 3–8.

William W. Herman, "Fathers: What Are You? Who Are You?" *Adolescence* (Spring, 1973), 139–49.

Elizabeth Herzog and Cecilia E. Sudia, "Fatherless Children," *Sexology*, (January, 1969), 428–430.

E. Mavis Hetherington, "Girls Without Fathers," *Psychology Today* 6 (1973), 47–52.

_____Martha Cox and Roger Cox, "Divorced Fathers," *Family Coordinator* 25 (October, 1976), 417–428.

_____"Divorced Fathers," *Psychology Today* 10 (April, 1977), 42–46.

Harry F. Keshet and Kristine M. Rosenthal, "Single-Parent Fathers," *Children Today* 7 (May-June, 1978), 13–19.

Sheila Fitzgerald Krein, "Growing Up In A Single-Parent Family: The Effect on Education and Earnings of Young Men," *Family Relations* Vol. 35, No. 1 (January, 1986), 161–168.

James A. Levine, *Who Will Raise the Children? New Options for Fathers and Mothers* (Philadelphia: Lippincott, 1976).

A. L. Milne, ed., *Joint Custody: A Handbook for Judges, Lawyers and Counselors* (Fort Lauderdale, Fla.: The Association of Family Conciliation Courts, 1979).

F. Ivan Nye and Felix M. Berado, "Changes in Husband and Father Roles," ed., Kenneth J. Scotte, *The Family: Its Structure and Interaction* (New York: MacMillan, 1973).

M. M. Polatnick, "Why Men Don't Rear Children: A Power Analysis," *Berkeley Journal of Sociology* 18 (1973), 142–146.

Barbara Riseman, "Can Men 'Mother'? Life as a Single Father," *Family Relations* Vol. 35, No. 1 (January, 1986), 95–111.

K. M. Rosenthal and H. Fl Keshet, *Fathers Without Partners* (Totowa, N.J.: Rowman and Littlefield, 1981).

_____"The Impact of Child Care Responsibilities on Part-time or Single Fathers—

Changing Patterns of Work and Intimacy," *Alternative Lifestyles* 1 (November, 1978), 465–491.

James Walters and Nick Stinnett, "Parent-Child Relationships: A Decade Review of Research," *Journal of Marriage and Family* Vol. 33 (1971), 70–111.

Chapter 5 and Chapter 6

C. J. Barrett, "Effectiveness of Widows' Groups in Facilitating Change," *Journal of Consulting and Clinical Psychology* 46 (1978), 20–31.

_____and K. M. Schneweis, "An Empirical Search for Stages of Widowhood," *Omega* 11 (1980–81), 97–104.

Felix M. Berado, "Survivorship and Social Isolation: The Case of the Aged Widower," *Family Coordinator* 19 (1973), 11–25.

Jane K. Burgess, "New Trends in Dating, Sexual Behavior, and Attitudes Toward Sex," Paper presented at a Singles' Conference, University of Wisconsin-Milwaukee (April, 1986).

_____and W. Kohn, *The Widower*, (Boston: Beacon Press, 1978).

_____"A Comparative Evaluation of the Pain and Coping Skills of Widowed and Divorced Men," in Rosanne Williams, et al. ed., *Family Strengths, Enhancements and Interaction* (Lincoln, Nebr.: The Department of Human Development and the Family, University of Nebraska, Lincoln, 1985).

Donn Byrne and William Griffitt, "Interpersonal Attraction," *Annual Review of Psychology* 24 (1973), 317–336.

Martha Cleveland, "Sexuality in the Middle Years," Peter J. Stein, ed., *Single Life* (New York: St. Martin's Press, 1981).

Marie Edwards and Eleanor Hoover, *The Challenge of Being Single* (New York: New American Library, 1974).

Erich Fromm, *The Art of Loving* (New York: Harper & Row Pub. Inc., 1956).

Carol D. Harvey and Howard Bahr, "Widowhood, Morale and Affiliation," *Journal of Marriage and the Family* 36 (1974), 97–106.

Clyde Hendrick and Susan Hendrick, *Liking, Loving, and Relating* (Monterey, Calif.: Brooks/Cole Pub. Co., 1983).

Dennis E. Hinkle and Michael J. Sporakowski, "Attitudes Toward Love: A Reexamination," *Journal of Marriage and the Family* 37 (1975), 764–767.

Morton Hunt, *The World of the Formerly Married* (New York: McGraw-Hill, 1966).

_____*Sexual Behavior in the 1970s* (New York: Dell, 1974a).

_____*Sexual Behavior of the 1970s* (Chicago: Playboy Press, 1974b).

_____and Bernice Hunt, *The Divorce Experience* (New York: McGraw-Hill, 1977).

Benjamin Kogan, *Human Sexual Expression* (New York: Harcourt Brace Jovanovich, 1973).

Mirra Komarovsky, "Cultural Contradictions and Sex Roles: The Masculine Case," *American Journal of Sociology* 78 (1973), 111–122.

Eda LeShan, *What Makes Me Feel This Way* (New York: Macmillan, 1972).

Roger W. Libby, "Creative Singlehood as a Sexual Lifestyle," in *Marriage and Alternatives: Exploring Intimate Relationships*, Roger W. Libby and Robert N. Whitehurst, eds., (Glenview, Ill.: Scott, Foresman and Company, 1977).

William Masters and Virginia Johnson, *Human Sexual Inadequacy* (Boston: Little, Brown and Co., 1970).

_____*Human Sexual Response* (Boston: Little, Brown and Co., 1966).

Stephen P. McCory and James L. McCory, *Human Sexuality*, 3rd edition, (Belmont, Calif.: Wadsworth, 1984).

C. M. Parkes, et al, "Broken Heart: A Statistical Study of the Increased Mortality Among Widowers," *British Medical Journal* (1969), 740–743.

_____and R. Brown, "Health After Bereavement: A Controlled Study of Young Boston Widows and Widowers," *Psychosomatic Medicine* 34 (1972), 449–461.

James Peterson and M. L. Bradey, *Widowers and Widowhood* (New York: Associated Press, 1977).

Carl R. Rogers, *Becoming Partners: Marriage and Its Alternatives* (New York: Delacorte, 1972).

L. B. Rubin, *Just Friends: The Role of Friendship in Our Lives* (New York: Harper & Row, 1985).

Constantina Safilios-Rothschild, *Love, Sex, and Sex Roles* (Englewood Cliffs, N.J.: Prentice-Hall, Inc. 1977).

Peter J. Stein, ed., *Single Life* (New York: St. Martin's Press, 1981).

Robert S. Weiss, "The Emotional Impact of Marital Separation," Peter J. Stein, ed., *Single Life* (New York: St. Martin's Press, 1981), 69–78.

_____"The Study of Loneliness," Peter J. Stein, ed., *Single Life* (New York: St. Martin's Press, 1981), 159–163.

R. B. Wey, ed., *Sexuality in the Later Years: Roles and Behavior* (New York: Academic Press, 1983).

Chapter 7

Sharon Albrecht, "Correlates of Marital Happiness Among the Remarried," *Journal of Marriage and the Family* (November, 1979), 857–867.

Gary S. Becker, E. Lanes, and R. Michael, "An Economic Analysis of Marital Instability," *Journal of Political Economy* 85 (1977), 1141–1187.

Paul Bohannan, *Divorce and After* (New York: Doubleday, 1970a).

_____"Divorce Chains, Households of Remarriage and Multiple Divorces," P. Bohannan, ed., *Divorce and After* (New York: Doubleday, 1970b), 127–139.

Andrew Cherlin, "Remarriage as an Incomplete Institution," *American Journal of Sociology* 84 (1978), 634–650.

W. Cleveland and D. Gianturco, "Remarriage Probability After Widowhood: A Retrospective Method," *Journal of Gerontology* 31 (1976), 99–103.

Frank F. Furstenberg, Jr. and Graham Spanier, "The Risk of Dissolution in Remarriage: An Examination of Cherlin's Hypothesis of Incomplete Institutionalization," *Family Relations* 33 (1984), 433–441.

Norval Glenn and Charles Weaver, "The Marital Happiness of Remarried Divorced Persons," *Journal of Marriage and the Family* 39 (1977) 331–337.

Paul Glick, "Remarriage: Some Recent Changes and Variations," *Journal of Family Issues* 1 (1980), 455–478.

_____and Arthur Norton, "Frequency, Duration and Probability of Marriage and Divorce," *Journal of Marriage and the Family* 33 (1971), 307–317.

Ann Goetting, "Former Spouse-Current Spouse Relationships,: *Journal of Family Issues* 1 (1980), 58–80.

_____"The Six Stations of Remarriage: Developmental Tasks of Remarriage After Divorce," *Family Relations* 31 (1982), 213–222.

J. McCarthy, "A Comparison of the Probability of Dissolution of First and Second Marriages," *Demography* 15 (1978), 345–359.

Jerry McKain, *Retirement Marriages* (Storrs, Conn.: Agricultural Experiment Station, Monograph 3, 1969).

_____"A New Look At Older Marriages," *Family Coordinator* 21 (1972), 61–69.

Lillian Messinger, "Remarriage Between Divorced People with Children from Previous Marriage," *Journal of Marriage and Family Counseling* 2 (1976), 193–200.

M. S. Moss and S. Z. Moss, "The Image of the Deceased Spouse in Remarriage of Elderly Widow(er)s," *Journal of Gerontological Social Work* 3 (1980), 59–69.

Leslie Aldridge Westoff, *The Second Time Around: Remarriage in America* (New York: Viking Press, 1977).

Chapter 9

The quotations cited in this chapter are from in-depth interviews conducted by the author of widowers, divorced, and involuntarily separated men.

M. J. Bane, *Here to Stay: American Families in the Twentieth Century* (New York: Basic Books, 1976).

C. J. Barrett, "Effectiveness of Widows' Groups in Facilitating Change," *Journal of Consulting and Clinical Psychology* 46 (1978), 20–31.

Felix M. Beradro, "Survivorship and Social Isolation: The Case of the Aged Widower," *Family Coordinator* 19 (1973) 11–25.

J. Bernard, *The Future of Marriage* (Middlesex, England: Penguin Harmondsworth, 1976).

B. L. Bloom, S. J. Asher & S. W. White, "Marital Disruption as a Stressor, A Review and Analysis," *Psychological Bulletin* (1978).

P. Bohannan, "The Six Stations of Divorce," in P. Bohannan, ed. *Divorce and After* (New York: Anchor Books, 1971).

E. M. Brown, "Divorce Counseling," in D.H.L. Olson, ed. *Treating Relationships* (Lake Mills, Iowa: Graphic Publishing, 1976), 394–429.

Jane K. Burgess & W. Kohn, *The Widower* (Boston: Beacon Press, 1978).

_____"A Comparative Evaluation of the Pain and Coping Skills of Widowed and Divorced Men," in Rosanne Williams, et al, ed., *Family Strengths 6, Enhancement of Interaction* (Lincoln, Nebr.: The Department of Human Development and the Family, University of Nebraska-Lincoln, 1985).

_____"The Widower as Father," in Shirley Hanson & F. W. Bozett, ed. *Dimensions of Fatherhood* (Beverly Hills: Sage Publications, 1985), 416–434.

N. D. Colletta, "Support Systems After Divorce: Incidence and Impact," *Journal of Marriage and the Family* 41 (1979), 837–846.

O. J. Coogler, *Structured Mediation in Divorce Settlement* (Lexington, Mass.: Lexington Books, 1978).

_____R. E. Weber and P. C. McKenry "Divorce Mediation: A Means of Facilitating Divorce and Adjustment," *Family Coordinator* 28 (April, 1979), 255–259.

P. Deckert and R. Langelier, "The Late-Divorce Phenomenon: The Causes and Impact of Ending 20-Year-Old or Longer Marriages," *Journal of Divorce* (Summer, 1978), 381–390.

Diana Dill and Ellen Feld, "The Challenge of Coping," in Deborah Belle, ed. *Lives and Stress* (Beverly Hills: Sage Publications, 1982), 179–196.

E. A. Dreyfus, "Counseling the Divorced Father," *Journal of Marital and Family Therapy* 5 (October, 1979), 79–85.

E. O. Fisher, "A Guide to Divorce Counseling," *Family Coordinator* 22 (January, 1973), 55–61.

S. Freud, "Mourning and Melancholia," J. Traviere, Trans. in *Collected Papers* Vol. 4 (New York: Basic Books, 1959).

I. O. Glick, R. S. Weiss & C. M. Parkes, *The First Year of Bereavement* (New York: Wiley, 1974).

W. R. Gove, "Sex, Marital Status and Morality," *American Journal of Sociology* 79 (September, 1973), 45–67.

J. M. Haynes, *Divorce Mediation* (New York: Springer, 1981).

M. S. Herrman, P. C. McKenry, and R. E. Weber, "Mediation and Arbitration Applied to Family Conflict Resolution: The Divorce Settlement," *Arbitration Journal* 34 (March, 1979), 17–21.

E. M. Hetherington, M. Cox and R. Cox, "The Aftermath of Divorce," in J. H. Stevens, Jr. and M. Mathews, eds. *Mother-Child, Father-Child Relations* (Washington D.C.: National Association for the Education of Young Children, 1978). 149–176.

Herbert H. Hyman, *Of Time and Widowhood* (Durham, N.C.: Duke Press, 1983).

G. F. Jacobson, *The Multiple Crises of Marital Separation and Divorce* (London: Grune and Stratton, 1983).

Richard H. Kalish, *Death, Grief and Caring Relationships* (Monterey, Calif.: Brooks/Cole Publ., 1985).

G. C. Kitson and M. B. Sussman, "The Impact of Divorce on Adults," *Conciliation Courts Review* (December, 1977), 20–24.

E. Lindeman, "Symptomatology and Management of Acute Grief," *American Journal of Psychiatry*, 101 (1944), 141–148. Reprinted in R. Fulton, ed. *Death and Identity* (New York: Wiley, 1965).

H. Z. Lopata, *Widowhood in an American City* (Cambridge, Mass.: Schenkman, 1973).

Deborah A. Luepnitz, *Child Custody: A Study of Families After Divorce* (Lexington, Mass.: Lexington Books, 1982).

Stephen P. McCary & James L. McCary, *Human Sexuality*, 3rd edition (Belmont, Calif.: Wadsworth, 1984).

Kari Moxnes, *His and Her Divorce*, Paper prepared for and presented at the 1986 NCFR Annual Conference, International Section, Detroit, Michigan.

I. Nye & F. M. Berardo, *The Family, Its Structure and Interaction* (New York: Macmillian, 1973).

C. M. Parkes, B. Benjamin, and R. G. Fitzgerald, "Broken Heart: A Statistical Study of Increased Mortality Among Widowers," *British Medical Journal* 1 (1969), 740–743.

_____"Determinants of Outcome Following Bereavement," *Omega* 6 (1975), 303–323.

_____& R. Brown, "Health After Bereavement: A Controlled Study of Young Boston Widows and Widowers," *Psychosomatic Medicine* 34 (1972), 449–461.

James Peterson & M. L. Briley, *Widows and Widowhood* (New York: Associated Press, 1977).

Robert A. Porter, "Crisis Intervention and Social Work Models," *Community Mental Health Journal* 2 (Spring, 1966), 17.

Lydia Rapoport, "Crisis-Oriented Short-Term Casework," *Social Service Review* 41 (March, 1967), 58.

K. M. Rosenthal & H. F. Keshet, *Fathers Without Partners* (Totowa, N.J.: Rowan and Littlefield, 1981).

G. B. Spanier and S. Hanson, "The Role of Extended Kin in the Adjustment to Marital Separation," Presented at the Annual Meetings of the Southern Sociological Society, New Orleans, Louisiana (1978).

U.S. Department of Commerce, Bureau of the Census, Current Population Reports, Consumer Income, Series P-60, No. 154 (1986).

J. Weinglass, K. Kressel, and M. Deutsch, "The Role of the Clergy in Divorce: An Exploratory Study," *Journal of Divorce* 2 (Fall, 1978), 57–82.

R. Weiss, "The Emotional Impact of Marital Separation," *Journal of Social Issues* 32 (Winter, 1976), 135–145.

_____*Marital Separation* (New York: Basic Books, 1975).

R. S. Wiseman, "Crisis Theory and the Process of Divorce," *Social Casework* 5 (Spring, 1975), 233–240.

Index

About the Author

JANE K. BURGESS is professor of sociology at the University of Wisconsin-Waukesha, where she has taught since 1967. She received her Ph.D. in 1972 from the University of Illinois at Champaign-Urbana. She has authored *The Widower* (1978), *Straight Talk About Love and Sex for Teenagers* (1979) published by Beacon Press, and numerous articles and chapters in books on the single-parent family, widowhood, divorce, the effects of death and/or divorce on the emotional development of children, and the relationship of the family to obesity. Recently she has written "The Widower as Father" in *Dimensions of Fatherhood*, published by Sage Publications in 1985.